Cambridge Elements ≡

Elements in New Religious Movements

Series Editor

Rebecca Moore

San Diego State University

Founding Editor

†James R. Lewis

Wuhan University

THE PRODUCTION OF ENTHEOGENIC COMMUNITIES IN THE UNITED STATES

Brad Stoddard

McDaniel College

T0311503

CAMBRIDGE
UNIVERSITY PRESS

CAMBRIDGE
UNIVERSITY PRESS

Shaftesbury Road, Cambridge CB2 8EA, United Kingdom

One Liberty Plaza, 20th Floor, New York, NY 10006, USA

477 Williamstown Road, Port Melbourne, VIC 3207, Australia

314–321, 3rd Floor, Plot 3, Splendor Forum, Jasola District Centre,
New Delhi – 110025, India

103 Penang Road, #05–06/07, Visioncrest Commercial, Singapore 238467

Cambridge University Press is part of Cambridge University Press & Assessment,
a department of the University of Cambridge.

We share the University's mission to contribute to society through the pursuit of
education, learning and research at the highest international levels of excellence.

www.cambridge.org
Information on this title: www.cambridge.org/9781009517409

DOI: 10.1017/9781009429412

© Brad Stoddard 2024

This publication is in copyright. Subject to statutory exception and to the provisions
of relevant collective licensing agreements, no reproduction of any part may take
place without the written permission of Cambridge University Press & Assessment.

When citing this work, please include a reference to the DOI 10.1017/9781009429412

First published 2024

A catalogue record for this publication is available from the British Library.

ISBN 978-1-009-51740-9 Hardback
ISBN 978-1-009-42940-5 Paperback
ISSN 2635-232X (online)
ISSN 2635-2311 (print)

Cambridge University Press & Assessment has no responsibility for the persistence
or accuracy of URLs for external or third-party internet websites referred to in this
publication and does not guarantee that any content on such websites is, or will
remain, accurate or appropriate.

The Production of Entheogenic Communities in the United States

Elements in New Religious Movements

DOI: 10.1017/9781009429412
First published online: June 2024

Brad Stoddard
McDaniel College

Author for correspondence: Brad Stoddard, bradlstoddard@gmail.com

Abstract: The rise of entheogenic religion – that is, religions that involve the use of psychoactive drugs – has captured the attention of scholars and journalists. These studies tend to advance the interests of practitioners who advocate for the legitimacy of entheogens and of entheogenic religion more broadly. This Element breaks with these approaches, as it offers a historical and critical analysis of entheogenic communities. It examines the production of entheogenic groups in the United States and considers the historical factors that have contributed to the rise in psychedelics more broadly. It also explores legal considerations and the impact of the law as a curator of entheogenic communities. This Element recognizes that these communities – like all imagined communities – are culturally conditioned, socially constructed, and historically contingent. By exploring these contingencies, we learn more about the broader sociocultural, historical, and economic frameworks that underlie the burgeoning association of psychoactive substances and religion.

Keywords: entheogens, psychedelics, religion, law

© Brad Stoddard 2024

ISBNs: 9781009517409 (HB), 9781009429405 (PB), 9781009429412 (OC)
ISSNs: 2635-232X (online), 2635-2311 (print)

Contents

Introduction

Brandi McGhee had a profound dream one night, that, as she interpreted it, called her to drink ayahuasca, a psychoactive "tea" long consumed by Indigenous people in the Amazon (Beyer 2009; Fotiou 2010; Labate & Jungaberle 2011).[1] This tea is banned in the United States because it contains N,N–Dimethyltryptamine (DMT), a substance classified as an illegal drug under the federal Controlled Substances Act (CSA), so Brandi followed this calling to a retreat center in Costa Rica, where she participated in her first ayahuasca ceremony. Like many others who consumed ayahuasca before her, she felt differently after the ceremony. Her mental health improved, she reevaluated her relationships, and she felt a deeper connection with her evolving spirituality. She also felt called to continue to work with ayahuasca, a calling that cost her friends and even her spouse. As Brandi described it, "You know, my entire life literally burned down and fell away so that this new life could be born."

Part of that new life included creating a new community in the United States centered on the ritual or sacramental consumption of ayahuasca. To create this community, Brandi consulted multiple attorneys, including Greg Lake and Ian Benouis, who provide legal counsel to help people form religious communities centered on the ritualistic consumption of psychoactive substances that in the United States are classified as illegal drugs. Under their advice, Brandi submitted paperwork with the state of Washington to create the New Birth Church, where Brandi and members of her congregation sacramentally consume ayahuasca.

Brandi's church is but one of the hundreds of communities in the United States today, where people gather to consume psychoactive substances like ayahuasca, psilocybin ("magic") mushrooms, peyote, and other substances that are commonly called "psychedelic drugs" (Lattin 2023). To distinguish themselves from people who consume these substances recreationally and to highlight the religious or spiritual aspects of their ceremonies and beliefs, they increasingly refer to their sacraments as "entheogens" instead of "psychedelics" or "drugs." Carl Ruck, a professor of classical studies at Boston University and advocate of psychedelic religion, coined this term in 1978 specifically to highlight the distinction between the recreational and the religious use of psychoactive substances (Wasson et al. 1978). The term has its share of critics

---

[1] Personal interview, conducted November 2021. At the request of the interviewee, "Brandi McGhee" is a pseudonym. She uses her real name on all her church's social media accounts, but she requested I create a pseudonym for her name and for her community.

(see Pollan 2018a), but it has not stopped tens of thousands of people from embracing the term to highlight their religiosity.[2]

Many entheogenic communities operate in private, as they attempt to avoid calling attention to themselves and risking arrest and even imprisonment. Communities like Brandi's, however, are hiding in plain sight. They file the paperwork to incorporate as churches, they have websites and social media pages, and they meet to consume psychoactive substances that are otherwise deemed illegal drugs under United States law. They tend to understand that they operate in legal gray areas of sorts, but based on interviews and casual conversations that I have conducted with dozens of people who formed these communities, they largely operate without fear of arrest and imprisonment.[3]

Brandi herself is not concerned about legal action because her attorneys informed her of several cases where the courts have granted to entheogenic communities exemptions from the generally applicable prohibition on psychoactive substances like ayahuasca. Her lawyers contend that in these cases, the courts have identified the criteria they will likely use to adjudicate similar exemptions in the future. By replicating these criteria and by staying within the boundaries of existing law, Brandi's lawyers contend that she is more likely to achieve favorable results if she is arrested or ends up in court.

In short, Brandi's lawyers maintain that these precedents bolster their client's legal legitimacy. These precedents however, also restrict Brandi's beliefs and practices, as she feels confined to imitate instead of innovate. As discussed in detail later in this Element, these precedents are outlined – at least according to entheogenic attorneys – in court cases like *United States* v. *Meyers* (1995), where a district court described common elements of religion, including various

---

[2] We should note that dominant terminology, including the terms psychedelics and entheogens, was created by white, male Americans, and that dominant histories of psychedelics center on the actions and influences of white men. This is important to note because, as I have argued elsewhere (Stoddard 2023), these histories omit or silence the voices of historical and contemporary actors who are not white males, despite their existence, contributions to, and roles in these histories. This is also important because women, nonbinary, and Black, Indigenous, and Other People of Color (BIPOC) contributors to psychedelic and/or entheogenic spaces largely embrace these terms, even as they alter them to advance local interests in these spaces and communities (for one example, see Jama-Everett 2021).

[3] The degree of fear is influenced by several factors, with race being perhaps the most significant factor. There is a large movement for BIPOC inclusivity in the broader entheogenic ecosystem, and BIPOC entheogenic users and their supporters are quick to highlight the racist history and aspects of the broader war on drugs. When BIPOC individuals create formal entheogenic communities, they are aware that in the event of any legal action initiated against them, the issue of race will be ubiquitous in any resulting proceedings. As I will discuss later in this Element, the issue of race and the racist aspects of the criminal justice system motivate some members of the BIPOC community to operate in the underground where they draw less attention than people who create formal and public-facing churches. When they do form public-facing churches, they are keenly aware that their race could result in additional burdens that white people will not necessarily face.

"accoutrements" of religion. By replicating religion as outlined in cases like *Meyers*, Brandi's lawyers contend that she will create "religion" in a manner already recognizable by courts.

In other words, Brandi and other entheogenic leaders today find themselves simultaneously empowered and constricted in a nation long known for religious innovation (Moore 1987). The tension between empowerment and innovation is the focus of this Element. Methodologically, this Element draws insights from scholars who have highlighted the various ways American laws create, define, and influence the production of religiosity in the United States (Jakobsen & Pelligrini 2003; Sullivan 2009; Sullivan 2014; Sullivan et al. 2015; Curtis 2016; Shakman Hurd & Sullivan 2021). Entheogenic communities like Brandi's exemplify this idea as these communities strive to exist within the boundaries of American law, even as they simultaneously push or test these boundaries.

This Element highlights the legal environment that simultaneously empowers and constricts entheogenic communities who strive for lawful legitimacy. I should state up front that this Element does not attempt to interpret the United States Constitution and related laws. Instead, it highlights and summarizes the history of the association of psychoactive substances and religiosity; it demonstrates how this association has always had legal, political, and sociocultural implications; it summarizes the evolving American legal environment related to the association of religiosity and illegal psychoactive substances; it analyzes interpretations of the Constitution and relevant legislation; and it explores the impact of court decisions on entheogenic communities.

Drawing from what is increasingly termed "critical religion," this Element begins with the assumption that dominant definitions of religion are new, historically contingent, and socially constructed (Martin 2014). Instead of normalizing sui generis religion, following the work of scholar Mitsutoshi Horii (Horii 2020), this Element examines the function of the category of religion within the broader intersections of American law and the resurging interest in psychedelics that has been termed the Psychedelic Renaissance (PR). We are often told that courts and state government protect religious freedom. This Element breaks with this assumption and instead explores how courts and governments regulate and quite literally produce religion.

To explore these dynamics, this Element briefly explores the changing associations of religiosity and psychoactive substances prior to the period of colonialism. It then summarizes various Christian responses to these associations within the broader context of colonialism. This history suggests, first, that Christian colonizers and their descendants have quite consistently leveraged to their benefit rhetorical and political arguments related to associations of religion and psychoactive substances. This history also demonstrates that these arguments are inherently political arguments with real-world implications. The overtly political implications of this history continue to be the focus of this Element as the discussion shifts to its primary focus, which is the work of attorneys Greg Lake and Ian Benouis.

Lake and Benouis are legal partners who have emerged as two of the most vocal and influential attorneys in the growing field of entheogenic law. They have helped many people create legal churches; they have spoken at psyche-delic conferences across the United States; individually and together, they have appeared on numerous podcasts; and they have consulted untold numbers of Americans who are in various stages of forming entheogenic communities. In a rather short period of time, they have emerged as leaders of the legal vanguard related to entheogenic communities. In this otherwise influential duo, however, Lake is particularly important, as he has published multiple books that address entheogens and the law (Lake 2021, 2022). This Element closely examines these books, as they summarize the ideas that underlie the legal advice and counsel that Lake and Benouis have provided to hundreds if not thousands of Americans.

Scholar of religion Winnifred Fallers Sullivan wrote that "New forms of religion require new forms of law" (Sullivan 2009, 18). Contemporary entheo-genic communities are increasingly recognized as new religions, and American courts are responding with new laws or with reinterpretations of existing laws and statutes. In this developing legal climate, attorneys like Lake and Benouis interpret these new legal decisions. By focusing on their activism, we learn, first, about the protean nature of religious freedom laws; second, about the reciprocal dialogue between the courts and entheogenic communities; third, about the dynamic limits of religious freedom; and finally, about the legal structures that sanction, discipline, and produce American religion.

As a result of this analysis, this Element demonstrates that the category of "new religious movements," a category long associated with what scholars (and society more broadly) consider new, emerging, or marginalized religious com-munities, is itself a political and legal category.[4] Groups that invoke the rhetoric of religiosity in new or innovative ways seek validation, recognition, and the legal and political protections and privileges that accompany the state's vali-dation of the group's religiosity. This validation requires groups to either conform to existing court-sanctioned models of religiosity or to challenge the courts to acknowledge novel forms of religiosity. This Element uses the example of

---

[4] Scholars who study new religious movements have long debated both the alleged object of study and the appropriate terms for the groups they study. This Element will not attempt to address this debate; rather, this analysis highlights how the categories themselves are constructed and arbitrary.

entheogenic communities to explore these dynamics, although this analysis is applicable to any group that scholars (and practitioners themselves) commonly label as new or emerging religions.

1 Origins Reconsidered: Rethinking the History of "Religion" and "Drugs"

As journalist Michael Pollan (2018a) noted in his bestselling book *How to Change Your Mind: What the New Science of Psychedelics Teaches Us About Consciousness, Dying, Addiction, Depression, and Transcendence*, psychedelic drugs are back and perhaps bigger than ever. Perhaps when most Americans think of psychedelic drugs, they think of the "psychedelic '60s"; the hippie movement or counterculture; and the saying "sex, drugs, and rock 'n' roll." In other words, many (possibly most) Americans associate psychedelic drugs with party culture and youthful rebellion. These associations are not entirely inaccurate, but as Pollan and others have documented, they are only part of the history of psychedelics in the United States.

As I will discuss in greater detail shortly, the history of psychedelics in North America predates colonialism, as some Native Americans consumed various psychoactive substances like peyote, a cactus that contains a psychoactive alkaloid called mescaline (Maroukis 2010), and psilocybin mushrooms (Jay 2019). It is particularly important to note that Native Americans consumed these substances, among other reasons, to interact with ancestors and with other supernatural entities. Native Americans did not, however, traditionally associate their activities with evolving notions of religion or religiosity, as (like all Indigenous peoples) they lacked a native term that corresponds to dominant definitions or notions of religion today. They also did not consume these substances in institutional churches, as the church model of social organization was similarly absent in precolonial societies and well into the colonial era. That began to change in the late 1800s. As white Americans decried the use of peyote and attempted to punish or persecute people who consumed peyote, Native Americans were increasingly exposed to white American culture, concepts, and models of social organization (Adams 1995). In the process, Native Americans began to adopt white Americans' terms like "religion" and "sacrament." They also considered the possibility of creating a formal church. In the process, Native Americans started to forge a new link between notions of religiosity and what are today called psychedelics.

The rhetoric of religiosity and its association with so-called psychedelic drugs expanded in the mid 1900s, when scholars and researchers explored both the religious aspects and the potential mental health benefits of LSD, mescaline, and psilocybin. These individuals were largely white Americans who, at least in the eyes of other white Americans, possessed more cultural capital than Native Americans. As a result, their invocations, associations, and interests carried more intellectual and cultural weight in the broader white American culture.

To understand this evolution, consider that in the 1950s and 1960s, many respected psychologists, psychiatrists, and public intellectuals like Huston Smith, Richard Alpert, and Aldous Huxley embraced psychedelics for their potential medical benefits, benefits primarily related to addiction, recovery, and mental health issues (Lattin 2017; Pollan 2018a). Psychologist and psychedelic activist Bill Richards described the optimistic spirit that surrounded psychedelic research in the 1960s when he said, "We thought [psychedelic research] was the most incredible frontier in psychiatry" (cited in Pollan 2018a, 58). This statement captures the enthusiasm that many researchers brought to the study of psychedelics before the war on drugs effectively ended psychedelic research, with Richards himself administering the last government-approved dose of psilocybin mushrooms in 1977 (Richards 2016, 4).

For several decades, interested parties shelved or suspended psychedelic research. That changed in the early 1990s, however, when psychiatrist Rick Strassman successfully petitioned the United States government to allow a researcher to resume psychedelic research (Strassman 2001). His research proved a harbinger of research to come, as government-approved psychedelic research has not only returned, but today is perhaps bigger than ever, as scholars in major universities have begun again to explore psychedelics' potential medical and religiospiritual benefits (see Griffiths et al. 2006). Their encouraging findings have motivated privately held and publicly traded companies to invest millions of dollars into psychedelic research (Phelps et al. 2022). Concurrently, therapists, psychologists, and social workers have embraced psychedelics as valuable adjuncts to therapy (Scheidegger 2021). While these professionals across various fields are espousing the virtues of psychedelics, cultural influencers like athletes, actors and actresses, and popular podcasters like Joe Rogan routinely describe allegedly beneficial results that accompany psychedelic experiences (Alahmari 2022). In short, psychedelics are occupying more space in various corners of the United States, and as psychedelics return closer to the American mainstream (premised largely on their potential medical or medicinal value), allegations of religious, spiritual, or mystical experience accompany this reappearance at almost every step.

We should immediately note that those in the broader entheogenic ecosystem – like people more broadly – have various and even competing definitions of the words religion, spirituality, mysticism, and entheogens. This malleability allows people to apply different labels to what appears to be similar rhetoric or descriptions of experiences, or conversely, to apply the same label to what appears to be a diversity of language and experience. Instead of endorsing any definition of these terms, this Element makes the competition over competing rhetoric and definitions an object of study.

While no one has conducted quantitative studies on what is commonly called psychedelic religion or entheogens in the United States, ethnographic research over the past three years suggests that more Americans are associating the consumption of "drugs" with religion or spirituality than at any point in US history. These consumers report religiospiritual experiences in various settings – ranging from individual sessions where they consume substances by themselves, in group sessions at retreat centers both in the United States and abroad, in research facilities, in therapeutic settings, in informal "circles," under the guidance of "tripsitters" and ceremony leaders, and in formal religious ceremonies held in entheogenic churches across the country (Lattin 2023). Regardless of the setting, people who consume psychoactive substances entheogenically often report that these substances engender or "occasion" mystical experiences, reveal metaphysical truths, connect the user with the supernatural, and allow users to interact directly with various entities or beings (Lutkajtis 2021; Shults 2022).[5] Based on these experiences, Americans are increasingly linking psychoactive substances like psychedelics and cannabis to their religious and spiritual lives.

Collectively, the work of researchers, businesses, and entheogenic activists combined to create what psychedelic activists and practitioners often call the Psychedelic Renaissance (PR), that is, the increased interest in and subsequent mainstreaming of psychedelics and other psychoactive substances targeted by the war on drugs.[6] As more people become interested in psychedelics today, they are reconsidering the history of psychedelics as well. To various degrees, these histories claim to document that the entheogenic use of psychedelics is ancient and near universal. Scholars and psychedelic activists have claimed to document entheogenic practices in ancient African religion (Duvall 2019), in

---

[5] The distinction between "inducing" or "engendering" and "occasioning" religious experience is an important distinction for many entheogenic consumers. The former terms, these consumers often say, imply that the entheogenic substance is the causal agent. Instead, they commonly argue that the entheogenic substance allows or occasions an experience with "that which exists independently" of the substance. From this latter perspective, "that which exists independently" is the cause of the experience, an experience the entheogenic substance "helps" or "occasions."

[6] As I will discuss later, the war on drugs began in earnest in the early 1970s during the presidency of Richard Nixon. As scholars have documented, this "war" resulted in longer prison sentences for more actions the government considered "crimes" (Pfaff 2017), specifically crimes related to drugs. This also resulted in the militarization of the police (Parenti 1999) and in the disproportionate incarceration of black Americans (Alexander 2010).

Hinduism (Kuddus et al. 2013), in various Indigenous religions in the Americas (Beyer 2009; Maroukis 2010), in Buddhism (Touw 1981; Badliner 2002; Osto 2016; Crowley 2019), in ancient Greek religion (Wasson et al. 1978), in ancient Judaism (Arie et al. 2020), in ancient Islam (Rosenthal 1971; Khalifa 1975), in the original Christian sacrament (Metzner 2005; Allegro 2009; Muraresku 2020), and in other traditions around the world (Wasson et al. 1986). Academically, these histories are often suspect, as they weave at times reliable histories with historical innuendo and speculative conjecture. While scholars can and should revisit and reevaluate these histories and historical narratives, Michael Pollan himself jokingly summarized the alleged prevalence of psychoactive substances in precolonial societies when he said, "this is something we do, and every culture on earth does it, with the one exception that proves the rule. The Inuit do not have any plant drugs, but it's only because none of them grow where they live. As soon as they go somewhere else, they get with the program" (Pollan 2018b).

Hyperbole aside, the fact remains that the historical, archaeological, and ethnographic data do suggest that psychoactive substances played and continue to play a larger role in more societies than perhaps most readers may imagine. From this perspective, the PR is not just connected to the 1960s; rather, its lineage extends thousands of years back in time to various corners of the globe (Wasson et al. 1986). The overt linkage between modern notions of religiosity and psychoactive substances, however, is a recent phenomenon.

Producing "Religious Drug Use"

As the previous summary suggests, activists and participants in the PR routinely link or associate religion or spirituality with the psychoactive substances that we commonly call drugs. Genealogists and historians of language, however, might highlight how these associations are contingent, historically conditioned, and tied to the intertwined legacies of colonialism, the Protestant Reformation, Native American sovereignty, and US jurisprudence. The history of this connection begins with evolving Christian notions of religiosity. As scholars have repeatedly documented, early Christians inherited the word *religio* and repeatedly modified its definition over roughly 1,500 years to suit their various and evolving interests (Smith 1982; Harrison 1990; Nongbri 2012). During this period, "religion" was a local or what scholars William Arnal and Russell McCutcheon termed a "folk taxonomy" that Christians used to highlight the differences between Christian *religion* and non-Christian beliefs and practices (Arnal & McCutcheon 2013). As scholar Peter Harrison observed, Christians within the context of the English Enlightenment began to question this distinction as they subsequently modified the word "religion" to highlight similarities Christians previously disputed (Harrison 1990). Specifically, they expanded the category of religion to include what they formerly classified as superstition or pagan. This expansion was but one part of what scholar Tomoko Masuzawa (2005) described as a larger intellectual intervention that resulted from European Christians who increasingly viewed and classified the world writ large though local taxonomies. According to Masuzawa, this larger movement served the interests of colonial powers and Euro-Christian dominance as it exported ideas and cultural concepts that ignored local taxonomies and that benefitted the colonial endeavor.

Christians spread and routinely modified this new and more inclusive version of "religion" within the context of colonialism as they selectively applied the category of religion to the people they encountered (Dirks 2001; Fitzgerald 2007; Chidester 2014). In short, due largely to the arbitrary fact that colonizers modified the concept of religion and theorized it as a universal concept, this is how many understand religion today.

As scholars, theologians, and Christians more broadly reevaluated notions of religiosity, they also reconsidered the relationship between the category of religion and the use of psychoactive substances. This will become particularly important for the history that this Element documents, as it demonstrates how dominant groups in the colonial context have used the category of religion to police the consumption of psychoactive substances. In other words, this history shows how entheogenic users today are connected to a much larger history where state actors (and the peoples who resist them) have deployed the idea of religion to either empower or to prohibit the use of psychoactive substances and to regulate the people who consume them.

For Christians, this history begins with the consumption of wine, a practice they inherited from their Greco-Roman and Jewish ancestors. Regarding the former groups, Greeks and Romans ritualistically consumed wine in all Mediterranean countries they conquered (Beltrán Peralta et al. 2022). Regarding the latter group, the Hebrew scriptures suggest that wine played an important role in ancient Hebrew societies, where Hebrews consumed it personally and ritualistically, occasionally drinking amounts that would induce at least mild if not overt intoxication (Jordan 2002). According to the Bible, Jesus embraced this tradition in the so-called Last Supper, where, as a Jew, he blessed bread and wine in a manner similar to the ritual blessing of wine and bread during Seder and Shabbat. His followers embraced this practice in the form of communion or the Eucharist, although monasteries routinely made either wine or beer for personal or group consumption outside the sacramental context (Beltrán Peralta et al. 2022). Protestant Reformer Martin Luther himself enjoyed beer, a fondness perhaps exaggerated by his critics (Roper 2010), but one that highlights a larger historical association of a psychoactive substance like alcohol with Christianity. Either way, the fact remains that as Christians colonized large parts of the world, they brought with them the idea that an intoxicating substance can either occasion or be used in conjunction with religious experience.

Christian colonizers had the opportunity to reconsider and potentially broaden this association, particularly in the Americas. In Mexico, Central America, and South America, colonizers encountered Indigenous populations who consumed psychoactive substances like psilocybin mushrooms, peyote, San Pedro, and ayahuasca (Letcher 2007; Beyer 2009; Dawson 2018; Jay 2019) – substances that in the United States and in many other countries today are called psychedelic drugs. While some colonizers expressed interest in these substances, the majority considered them to have a diabolical nature and cited the Indigenous use of these substances to justify the colonial endeavor. In 1653, for example, Spanish priest and Jesuit missionary Bernabé Coco observed Indigenous Peruvians who used San Pedro (a psychoactive cactus containing mescaline) and wrote, "this is the plant with which the Devil deceived the Indians of Peru in their paganism ... transported by this drink, the Indians dreamed a thousand absurdities and believed them as if they were true" (see Jay 2019, 25). Roughly three decades earlier, the Holy Office of the Spanish Inquisition banned peyote use based on similar logic (Labate & Cavnar 2016, xxi). Christian immigrants and their descendants in the United States did not pass a federal ban on these substances until the 1900s, but they reached similar conclusions about the relationship between peyote and the devil (Dawson 2018).

Theoretically, one can imagine scenarios where Christian colonizers might have accepted or even embraced these substances and either integrated them into Christianity or classified the consumption of these substances as religious. Instead, Christians routinely denied these linkages and persecuted people who consumed these substances. The question remains – why? Scholar Petter Grahl Johnstad attempted to answer that question when he argued that racial and religious motives are perhaps the primary factors motivating opposition to so-called drugs (Johnstad, 2023). These factors persisted during the colonial era and beyond.

As this suggests, colonizers erected boundaries between psychoactive substances. They deemed wine a sacrament capable of being consumed within the context of religious rituals. When they encountered psychoactive substances like peyote and San Pedro, however, they created a taxonomic distinction for these substances, which they commonly labeled as diabolical or poison. In other words, Christian colonizers in the colonial era did not deny the linkage between religiosity and psychoactive substances; rather, they policed this linkage as they only considered it within the context of Jewish and Christian traditions.[7] This denial functioned to serve colonial economic interests, as it, in the minds of colonizers, provided additional ideological justifications for the larger colonial project, premised on the capturing of land, people, and the wealth that accompanied colonialism.

Challenging the Colonial Paradigm

In the late 1900s, Native Americans would force the American legal system to revisit the relationship between religion and the consumption of psychoactive substances. To understand this history, consider that while the historical record is limited, documents and oral traditions combine to suggest that for thousands of years, some Native Americans in northern Mexico and in the southern regions of bordering states ritualistically consumed a psychoactive cactus called peyote (Dawson 2018). They dried and processed peyote to make a tea, which they drank as a form of medicine and as a vehicle to induce or occasion supernatural experiences and interactions with ancestors and various entities or gods. Peyote rituals spread in the 1800s, particularly among Native Americans confined to reservations, as the consumption of peyote increasingly became a marker of an evolving pan-Indian identity. Many Native Americans denounced the practice, but their dissent did not prevent the consumption of peyote from spreading. For their part, white Americans typically condemned the use of peyote as they again associated it with diabolical influence (Maroukis 2010), and several states passed legislation to ban peyote. Peyote's critics sought a similar federal ban, but they would not achieve their intended goals in the 1800s.

As the use of peyote grew among Native Americans in the late nineteenth century, it caught the attention of James Mooney (1861–1921), a young ethnologist turned supporter of Native Americans, who in 1896, published an account of his experience of a peyote ritual (Mooney 1896). Challenging the Americans who decried the use of peyote, Mooney described peyote as overtly religious when he wrote, "the ceremonial eating of the plant has become the great religious rite of all of the tribes of the southern plains" (compare Maroukis 2010, 29). To help Native Americans advocate for their ability to consume peyote, Mooney suggested that Native Americans create a formal church based on the sacramental consumption of peyote. As a white American versed in

---

[7] Scholar Aaron Hughes (2012) discussed various problems with the notion of "Abrahamic Religions." His insights apply as well to the concept of "Judeo-Christian."

American culture and law, Mooney knew that the words "religion" and "sacrament" invoked both sociocultural and legal capital. Mooney also knew the formal institutional structure of a church would present "religion" in a form that white Christians would more likely recognize. By creating a church and invoking these concepts, Mooney believed this linkage would help bolster Native Americans' arguments to legally consume peyote. The problem was that this particular language and administrative structure were foreign to Native Americans. The impulse to create a Native American church illustrates this Element's central argument. Specifically, multiple factors combine to influence and to quite literally produce religiosity in forms recognizable to the US political and legal systems. These forms are not natural and instead reflect the expectations of the relevant power structures, structures tied to the modern nation state (Mahmood 2015).

Native Americans eventually followed Mooney's advice and incorporated the Native American Church of Oklahoma (NAC) in 1918. Scholars often describe NAC as a church that blended elements of Christianity and Native American religion centered on the ritualistic consumption of peyote. As one example of this hybridity, NAC's founding charter called peyote both a teacher, and more importantly, a sacrament (Maroukis 2010, 126). The founding of NAC is important because NAC's founders, like Mooney, recognized that they were asking white America to modify the taxonomic structure of "religion," which viewed religiosity and the consumption of substances like peyote as incompatible. They also recognized the legal implications of their beliefs and practices, and unconsciously or not, they believed that the rhetoric of religiosity would potentially bolster their political and legal positions.

The founders of the NAC failed, however, to persuade the majority of white Americans of the religiosity of their Christian-influenced peyote rituals. In 1923, for example, G. E. E. Lindquist (1886–1967), a Christian missionary to Native Americans considered by white Americans to be an authority on Native Americans, wrote *The Red Man in the United States*, in which he described what he repeatedly called "the peyote cult" and where he spoke disparagingly of peyote ceremonies and of Native Americans' adaptations and modifications of his own brand of Christianity (Wenger 2009). Lindquist also quoted fellow missionary, Rev. Henry Vruwink (1886–1969), who described peyote as inherently opposed to Christianity. According to Vruwink, "The ignorant Indian may and does put peyote in the place of the Bible; in the place of the Gospel; in the place of the Holy Spirit" (cf. Lindquist 1923, 74). Lindquist endorsed a similar position when he wrote, "[the peyote ceremony] is a false worship carried on under the guise of Christian teachings. It is utterly destructive of morals, health and fellowship in the Christian Church and in the nation" (75). Collectively,

Lindquist and Vruwink represent a common response to the NAC, demonstrating that its appeal to religiosity failed to win the day in the court of public opinion. The members of NAC would eventually realize their goals, but that victory would prove many decades away.

While Native Americans continued to advocate for the religious use of peyote, scholar William James (1842–1910) entered and influenced the debate more broadly. In the early 1900s, James was an accomplished philosopher, psychologist, and theorist of religion (Myers 2001; Richardson 2006). He delivered a series of lectures at Edinburgh University, which were subsequently published in 1902 titled *The Varieties of Religious Experience*. In *Varieties*, James juxtaposed individualized and experience-based religion with institutional religion. He advocated quite strongly for the former. As a perennialist who believed that pure and authentic religious experience is ultimately the same regardless of the tradition that helps manifest the experience, James wanted to describe the universal characteristics of religious experience, focusing extensively on mystical experience, which he considered one type of religious experience. To that end, James analyzed and cited mystics from various traditions. Based on his interpretation of their practices, James concluded that mystical experience has four components: noetic (associated with the acquisition of knowledge), ineffable (difficult to describe), passive (the mystic feels as if their will were under the influence of a superior power), and transient (temporary or difficult to sustain for long periods of time) (James 1902, 380–2).

Having identified what he considered the universal characteristics of mysticism, James applied these insights to his own experiences with nitrous oxide (also known as laughing gas), a psychoactive gas that induces an altered state for roughly one minute. Reflecting on this experience, James wrote,

> One conclusion was forced upon my mind at that time, and my impression of its truth has ever since remained unshaken. It is that our normal waking consciousness, rational consciousness as we call it, is but one special type of consciousness, whilst all about it, parted from it by the filmiest of screens, there lie potential forms of consciousness entirely different. (James 1902, 388)

James continued to argue that nitrous oxide induced a mystical experience, and by extension of his logic, he concluded that other psychoactive substances can occasion similar experiences. James described this when he wrote, "The next step into mystical states carries us into a realm that public opinion and ethical philosophy have long since branded as pathological, though private practice and certain lyric strains of poetry seem still to bear witness to its ideality. I refer to the consciousness produced by intoxicants and anaesthetics, especially by alcohol" (James 1902, 386–7). In other words, James asserted a much larger relationship between religious mystical experience and psychoactive substances, one that would arguably include substances like peyote, San Pedro, and other "drugs" condemned by the wider society as antithetical to religion and religiosity. In the process, James created an intellectual argument, first, that resonated with Native Americans' claims about peyote, and second (as evidenced by the people who later consumed psychedelics and who cited James' work), that would convince more people in the United States and beyond to accept a broader link between religion and what many people could consider "drugs." This was a significant intellectual intervention, one that would become important, and politically salient, decades later within the context of the 1960s counterculture or hippie movement, where young Americans increasingly consumed "drugs" and associated them with religiosity, spirituality, or mystical experience.

To understand this history, consider that in a rather short period of time, several psychoactive agents were introduced into and circulated through parts of American society. As early as 1918, a scientist synthesized mescaline, the psychoactive ingredient in peyote and San Pedro (Jay 2019). Decades later, mescaline circulated in pill form as psychologists and psychiatrists explored the drug's potential medical value, primarily related to mental health. Additionally, in 1957, many Americans became aware of psilocybin mushrooms after R. Gordon Wasson (1898–1986), a banker and amateur mycologist, ceremonially consumed mushrooms in Mexico. Wasson published an account of his experiences in *Life Magazine*, where over the course of fifteen pages, which included multiple photos, he described the experience, specifically highlighting the religious aspects of the ceremony. Wasson wrote,

> On the night of June 29–30, 1955, in a Mexican Indian village so remote from the world that most of the people still speak no Spanish, my friend Allan Richardson and I shared with a family of Indian friends a celebration of "holy communion" where "divine" mushrooms were first adored and then consumed. (Wasson 1957, 101)

Wasson continued to describe the ceremony in detail as he spoke favorably of the experience and described it as an enlightening and overtly sacred or religious event.

As a result of this publication, in a short period of time, millions of Americans learned, first, of psychoactive mushrooms, and second, that the Indigenous people who consumed these substances associated them with religion and religiosity. People in the evolving field of mental health took notice of psilocybin mushrooms and began to investigate them as well, keenly aware that in addition to whatever medical or mental health benefits these substances might provide, associations of religious experience tended to accompany their use.

In addition to mescaline and psilocybin, however, it was LSD that became most famously and infamously associated with the 1960s counterculture (Lee & Shlain 2007). Chemist Albert Hofmann (1906–2008) first synthesized LSD, or lysergic acid diethylamide, during a series of ergot experiments in 1938. Sensing no value to the liquid, he literally shelved it. As Hofmann later described, he continued to have a nagging sense that it might be useful, so several years later, he resumed his research (Hofmann 2009). While researching LSD in 1943, Hofmann accidentally splashed some LSD on his skin, and subsequently experienced the world's first LSD trip, an experience that he described as "not unpleasant" (Hofmann 1980, 15). Curious to explore further, three days later, he deliberately ingested it on April 19, 1943. This experience, however, was different. Hofmann later wrote that this experience "revealed LSD in its terrifying, demonic aspect" (Hofmann 1980, 17). Based on his experiments, Hofmann argued that LSD was unique and that it possessed medical value. "I was aware that LSD," he wrote, "a new active compound with such properties, would have to be of use in pharmacology, in neurology, and especially in psychiatry, and that it would attract the interest of concerned specialists" (Hofmann 1980, 17). Hofmann was correct.

Sensing that LSD might help psychologists and psychiatrists understand mental health disorders, Sandoz, the company for which Hofmann worked, created thousands of LSD doses and shipped them around the world to just about anyone willing to experiment with LSD. In the process, researchers added LSD to the list of "psychedelics" (meaning "mind manifesting"), a term that a British psychologist coined in 1957 (Osmond 1961, 76).

On the eve of the 1960s counterculture, scholars and researchers continued to research and to write about the potential benefits of psychedelics. As Pollan noted, by 1965, their research resulted in more than 1,000 publications in academic journals. The academic and counterculture's interest in psychedelics combined to suggest that psychedelics were poised to revolutionize America's understanding of mental health, religiosity, and spirituality. A series of factors, however, combined to thwart the interests of psychedelic activists and enthusiasts.

2 Psychedelic Religion in the Era of Prohibition

On the cusp of the 1960s, an informed person might have reasonably concluded that psychedelics were on the brink of ushering in a new era of psychological insights premised on the consumption of psychoactive substances that seemed to involve or invoke religious experience. Researchers and proponents thought as much. A series of factors, however, would combine to stifle their efforts and steer the country in a new and historically unprecedented era of prohibition based on the idea that psychedelics possessed no medical value and were instead dangerous drugs that should be regulated and forbidden under force of law. A brief summary will help highlight this transition, psychedelics' evolving association with religion, and the legal landscape that made psychedelic religiosity a more politically salient topic.

When scholars discuss psychedelics' transition from respectability to prohibition, they commonly focus on Timothy Leary (1920–1996), a young and promising psychologist in the late 1950s who embraced psychedelics and whom many Americans eventually viewed as the prime example for everything wrong with psychedelics. Popular lore commonly contends that President Richard Nixon once called Leary "the most dangerous man in America," and scholars and historians have repeated this claim (see Lattin 2012, 217).[8] Apocryphal or not, however, whether Nixon actually said these words, the statement accurately captures the contempt that many mainstream Americans developed for Leary, whom they saw as the self-proclaimed messiah, leader, guru, or high priest of the 1960s counterculture (Leary 1968). We should note that Leary was not single-handedly responsible for taking psychedelics out of the laboratories and into the streets. He did, however, play a large role in spearheading the transition from respectability to prohibition, and he is a useful figure that symbolizes and embodies this transition. Additionally, and more germane to the subject of this Element, Leary is particularly important to the subsequent history of overt linkages of psychedelics and religiosity.

To understand this history, consider that in 1950, Leary completed his Ph.D. in clinical psychology at the University of California, Berkeley (Greenfield 2006; Higgs 2006). He continued his psychological pursuits both inside and outside academia, developing a modest reputation as a contrarian thinker. His ideas and activities captured the attention of colleagues at Harvard University, which in 1959, hired Leary as a lecturer. Like many psychologists before him, Leary ingested mescaline, psilocybin, and LSD. He became convinced that these substances could help advance the field of psychology and our understanding of the human mind more broadly.

To explore these substances, Leary partnered with fellow Harvard psychologist Richard Alpert (1931–2019), and from 1960 to 1962 they administered the

---

[8] Scholars have not been able to verify that Nixon actually said this (Gunther 2020).

Harvard Psilocybin Project (HPP, see Lattin 2010). Harvard granted Leary the authority to perform experiments on graduate students involving psilocybin mushrooms. Leary was originally interested in psilocybin's psychological benefits, but participants often described their experiences as religious, spiritual, or mystical (Leary et al. 1964). Alpert himself explicitly connected the HPP to James when he described their work as "right in the tradition of William James" (cited in Pollan 2018a, 196). As more participants reported mystical or religious experiences, the religious aspects of psychedelics increasingly consumed Leary's interests. Pollan captured Leary's mindset when he wrote, "It had become clear to [Leary] that the spiritual and cultural import of psilocybin and LSD far outweighed any therapeutic benefit to individuals" (Pollan 2018a, 192).

To unambiguously explore the religious aspects of psilocbyin, Walter Pahnke (1931–1971), a minister and graduate student under Leary's guidance, conducted the so-called Marsh Chapel or Good Friday experiment (Pahnke 1963). In this experiment, Pahnke gathered twenty students from a local divinity school and administered psilocybin to half the participants and a placebo to the other half. Pahnke then asked participants to complete a mysticism scale that allegedly ranked the degree to which the subject had an authentic mystical experience. Based on their responses, Pahnke concluded that almost everyone who received psilocybin had a mystical experience, compared to only one person who received the placebo. These findings combined with Leary's research, previous scholarship, and the testimonies of Native Americans to highlight psychedelics' alleged ability to occasion the religious experiences that mystics for thousands of years and from various parts of the globe labored years or decades to achieve. In other words, the Marsh Chapel Experiment added intellectual fuel to the argument that psychoactive substances can induce or occasion spiritual experience. The problem for Leary, Pahnke, and other proponents of psychedelic-related religiosity, however, was that the public narrative on psychedelics was about to change.

While Leary and his broader team explored the various aspects of psychedelics, Leary's critics kept a close eye on him (Lattin 2010). They complained that his experiments included undergraduate students and that these experiments often resulted in drug-fueled orgies. Harvard responded by terminating Leary's contract and by firing Alpert. Their dismissal was but one symbol and symptom of a larger transition as psychedelics left the laboratory and entered a counterculture that rejected mainstream and traditional American values. Simultaneously, many Americans began to sour on psychedelics. Public campaigns espoused the dangers of psychedelics and people reported crimes, murders, and even suicides associated with these substances. People like Leary correctly feared that a national ban was inevitable.

Leary and likeminded psychedelic users increasingly faced both a sociocultural and political problem. They believed in the transformative power of psychedelics premised on religious or mystical experience; however, their sacraments were being criminalized. With prohibition looming, Leary replicated a strategy Native Americans previously pursued when he highlighted the religiosity of psychedelic use. In 1962, Leary formed the International Federation for Internal Freedom, the first of several religions that he would create and lead, including the Castalia Foundation and later the League for Spiritual Discovery, or LSD. Additionally, in 1967 he wrote *Start Your Own Religion*, a comparably short book that was part instruction manual designed to convince young people to "turn on, tune in, and drop out." It documented the creation of the League for Spiritual Discovery and outlined Leary's vision and rationale for psychedelic churches. Regarding the latter, Leary explicitly addressed "The Legal Question," when he argued that "The First Amendment to the Constitution, the Charter of the U.N., and the ancient traditions of human history give you protection to alter your own consciousness inside your shrine" (Leary 1967, 11). "YOU ARE GOD," he wrote. "REMEMBER!"

Unintentionally or not, Leary recognized that religious freedom might be psychedelic religion's savior, and he was prepared to (at least modestly) play by the government's rules. Despite his apparent acquiescence, however, Leary made clear his contempt for the government. To this end, borrowing biblical language, Leary condemned the state, which he repeatedly called Caesar (Leary 1967, 11), but he also recognized the reach of the state and its ability to criminalize behaviors and to punish transgressors. "For both psychedelic and legal reasons," he wrote, "you must form your own cult" (Leary 1967, 5). In short, Leary's writings, speeches, and actions suggest he had a heartfelt belief in the spiritual potential of psychedelics, but they also indicate that he possessed the political savvy to understand that in the face of imminent prohibition, the frame of "religion" provided a potential justification for the continued use of psychedelics in an era increasingly inhospitable to these substances. This justification would involve restrictions, but Leary seemed willing to accept them, provided the government granted him the right to consume psychedelics.

Despite his efforts, Leary never achieved his more ambitious goal of success-fully lobbying the government to officially sanction psychedelic religion. Instead, in 1970 the federal government outlawed all psychedelics in the Controlled Substances Act (CSA). Prohibition was now the law of the land. Over the next several decades, the US government increasingly waged its now famous (and increasingly infamous; see Baum 1996) war on drugs. This war consisted of various factors, beginning with the government classifying certain substances as drugs and subject to regulation and criminalization. The government then classified these drugs under various schedules depending on their alleged potential for abuse, potential for addiction, safety, and the substances' medical use. Psychedelics were classified as Schedule I drugs, meaning the government classified them as having no medical use and a high likelihood of abuse and addiction. The United States waged this war at home, where it relied on a newly and increasingly militarized police force to enforce the war on drugs (Parenti 1999). This resulted, first, in longer and more draconian sentences for drug offenders (Garland 2001; Useem & Piehl 2008), and second, in the disproportionate incarceration of African Americans (Alexander 2010; Muhammad 2010; Schoenfeld 2018). The United States exported the war on drugs to other countries and to international governing bodies, which similarly mobilized state and military resources to fight drugs. As a result, many people stopped using psychedelics and state-sanctioned psychedelic research ceased to exist (see Richards 2016).

Not everyone, however, abandoned the use of psychedelics. In the United States and beyond, many people risked their freedom to continue to use psychedelics. Instead of disappearing, psychedelics were confined largely to the underground, where people continued to use them for recreational and religious purposes. Some people followed Leary's lead and created churches premised on the sacramental consumption of psychedelics and cannabis. As independent historian Mike Marinacci (2023) documented, in the wake of prohibition, many people formed psychedelic religions like The Church of the Awakening, The Peyote Way Church of God, The Neo-American Church, and The Shiva Fellowship, to name just a few. Collectively, the founders of these churches saw in religious freedom laws a potential vehicle for challenging prohibition. As Marinacci noted, some of these churches and their leaders avoided legal encounters or entanglements, but some people ended up in court where they lost case after case. The founders and members of these communities hoped to find solace in the First Amendment's commitment to religious freedom. Instead, they found themselves on the losing end of multiple court battles where judges repeatedly rejected their legal theories (Marinacci 2023). In short, it became clear that religious practice claims would not shield people from the generally applicable prohibition on psychedelics and cannabis. In this otherwise consistent legal milieu in the 1980s, Native Americans soon emerged to once again challenge the legal paradigm that had beleaguered them for over a century. Their challenges would impact psychedelic religion more broadly.

Peyote Religion Goes to Court

In 1990, the US Supreme Court decided what would become a momentous and controversial case. This case, *Employment Division* v. *Smith*, began with Alfred Smith and Galen Black, both of whom were members of the Native American Church. Both men also worked at a drug rehabilitation clinic, which tested the men's urine and found evidence of mescaline. Based on the company's zero-tolerance policy for drugs, the company fired both men for violating company policies. The men soon filed for employment compensation on the grounds that they were dismissed for exercising their religious rights. The question emerged: Were the men wrongfully terminated for practicing their religion or was the dismissal justifiable because the men violated a generally applicable law? After a series of lower court decisions, the US Supreme Court heard the case. Based on precedent, most people watching the case expected the court to apply the doctrine of strict scrutiny, which contends that the government should not substantially burden a person's exercise of religion unless there is a compelling governmental reason, in which case the offending law should be narrowly tailored to least restrict the exercise of religion. Should the court apply this doctrine, most scholars and legal analysts expected the court to side with Smith (Parsell 1992).

In a surprise decision, however, the court did not apply strict scrutiny and denied the men's request for unemployment compensation on the grounds that drug prohibition was a generally applicable law that did not specifically target religion (Hutchison 2022). This decision was important, not only because it overturned existing precedent (Lupu 1993), but because it seemed to settle the debate over the legality of psychedelic or entheogenic religion. Roughly one hundred years earlier, Native Americans asserted that religious freedom gave them the right to consume a psychoactive substance that was illegal in several states and jurisdictions. Leary and likeminded people made similar arguments in the 1960s and beyond. *Employment Division* v. *Smith* seemingly settled the issue when the court concluded that Americans do not possess a constitutional right to consume illegal psychoactive substances for religious reasons. Legally speaking, this would have effectively ended the debate over the legality of religious drug use. Subsequent legislation, however, would soon resuscitate it.

In the otherwise hyperpartisan 1990s political climate, the *Smith* decision united people from diverse coalitions in opposition to the court (see Pavlik 1992). Journalist Kelsey Dallas described this diversity as "Democrats and Republicans, evangelicals and Muslims, The Church of Jesus Christ of Latter-day Saints and the ACLU, and many, many other groups willing to put aside their political and religious differences to strengthen legal protections for people of faith" (Dallas 2023). According to law professor Marci Hamilton, there are several factors that motivated this increasingly organized opposition (Hamilton 2005). Chief among them, various politicians and religious and political actors misread the *Smith* decision, misunderstood precedent, and misunderstood the impact of *Smith* (225–6). Additionally, the *Smith* decision resonated with Republicans who previously complained of the erosion of religious liberty (primarily as it related to Christians and Christianity), and it resonated with Democrats' concerns that the *Smith* decision was the latest government intrusion on Native Americans' rights and traditions. The "fix," these groups argued, was new congressional legislation.

To this end, in 1993 then-Congressman Chuck Schumer introduced into Congress a bill titled the Religious Freedom Restoration Act (RFRA). RFRA is a relatively short and succinct bill that contains three elements, or prongs. In language reminiscent of strict scrutiny, RFRA contends that the "Government shall not substantially burden a person's exercise of religion even if the burden results from a rule of general applicability" unless – the second prong – there is a "compelling governmental interest" or reason (42 U.S.C. § 2000bb–1[a]). The third prong or element of RFRA veers subtly but importantly from the previous precedent when it states that in the event of a compelling governmental interest to substantially burden the exercise of religion, the government shall take "the least restrictive means of furthering that compelling governmental interest." In other words, strict scrutiny called for the government to "narrowly tailor" laws that restrict religion, whereas RFRA shifted the burden to the government to take the "least restrictive means" of substantially burdening religion (see Hamilton 2005). With the support of Republicans and Democrats, RFRA sailed through Congress and President Bill Clinton signed it into law on November 16, 1993.

The Impulse to bolster religious freedom did not end with RFRA, as evidenced by the Religious Land Use and Institutionalized Persons Act of 2000 (RLUIPA – see Lupu and Tuttle 2011). RLUPIA resembles RFRA in several ways. First, it is congressional legislation designed to create a firmer legal foundation for religious freedom. Additionally, the text of RLUIPA resembles RFRA's text with a few notable exceptions. Where RFRA was designed to protect religious freedom for Americans writ large, RLUIPA – absent a compelling governmental interest – protects religious institutions from zoning and landmarking laws that substantially burden religious institutions or organizations. It also prevents the government from substantially burdening the religiosity of people institutionalized in government-controlled spaces like prisons. If there is a compelling governmental interest, the government must take the least restrictive means of furthering that compelling governmental interest.

Like RFRA, Congress enthusiastically endorsed RLUIPA (it passed without objection in the House and passed unanimously by the Senate) and was signed into law by then-President Clinton on September 22, 2000.[9] Individually and together, RLUIPA and RFRA reflect a growing trend to use the federal government to protect religious freedom (Meier 2007).

RFRA was a clear response to the court's decision in the *Smith* case; however, the text of RFRA does not mention Alfred Smith, Native Americans, or peyote. Instead, RFRA was a broad endorsement of religious freedom. Native Americans and their supporters were keenly aware that RFRA seemed to sidestep the issue of peyote, so they continued to lobby for additional action. Congress responded in 1994 by amending the American Indian Religious Freedom Act (AIRFA) of 1978 to explicitly grant Native Americans the right to consume peyote in religious settings. In other words, for the first time since the prohibition of alcohol, the federal government allowed a specific group of people to use an otherwise illegal psychoactive substance for religious reasons. The question remained, however: Do any entheogenic communities have standing under RFRA to consume otherwise illegal drugs?

The subsequent history of RFRA is complex (see Neuman 1997; Laycock 2018), but several aspects of RFRA are worth considering. Despite the overwhelming support for RFRA, the law developed its share of critics. As evidenced by Hamilton's (2005) important book *God vs. the Gavel*, some of the law's critics contended that RFRA can result in harm, primarily to children and other vulnerable populations who might be victimized by religious people and groups that would benefit from the government's deference to religion. Additionally, scholars like James Richardson and Barbara McGraw (2019) voiced concern that RFRA would result in discrimination against women and members of the LGBT community. They were also concerned that religious people could leverage RFRA to attack issues related to the "sexual rights" movement more broadly. Scholar Andrew Lewis summarized RFRA's potential impact as one piece of a larger movement to make religious rights the penultimate rights, even at the expense of other notions of civil or public rights (Lewis 2017).

Concerns over RFRA's peripheral impact developed in earnest several decades after its passage. More immediately, however, some critics argued that RFRA exceeded Congress's ability to effectively overturn a Supreme Court decision (Eisgruber & Sager 1994; Hamilton 1998). These critics soon had

---

[9] For a criticism of RLUIPA, see Walsh 2001 and Osborn 2004.

their day in court – ultimately in the Supreme Court – in 1996's *City of Boerne* v. *Flores*. The details of this case are not particularly relevant to this Element, but the case's impact is quite important (Laycock 1998). In *Flores*, a majority of the court's justices concluded that RFRA is an unconstitutional violation of states' rights and therefore does not apply to state laws. The question remained, however: Did RFRA apply to federal laws?

Ayahuasca Religion Goes to Court

Entheogenic users and communities were particularly interested in the preceding question. If the US Supreme Court concluded that RFRA was unconstitutional in its entirety, entheogenic users and communities effectively had no legal recourse under the law. Conversely, if the Supreme Court ruled that RFRA did apply to laws created by the federal government, entheogenic users and communities saw a narrow legal window to potentially bolster their ability to be exempt from the generally applicable law that is drug prohibition. As history soon demonstrated, the Supreme Court addressed these issues in *Gonzales* v. *O Centro Espírita Beneficente União do Vegetal* (546 U.S. 418, 2006).

In theory, any religious freedom claim related to federal laws could have considered the legality of RFRA, but the specific case that ultimately addressed this issue was one that involved another entheogen. This particular case involved ayahuasca, the psychoactive "tea" or drink discussed at the beginning of this Element. As we recall, ayahuasca is illegal in the United States because it contains DMT, which the CSA classified as an illegal Schedule I drug, meaning that the government considers it a dangerous drug with no medical use and a high potential for abuse. Indigenous people in the Amazon have consumed ayahuasca for thousands of years, but as we will address in detail later in this Element, several ayahuasca churches developed in Brazil in the 1900s and came to North America in the 1990s (Labate & Jungaberle 2011). Despite the CSA, the founders of these communities imported ayahuasca and served it to church members. Two of these churches would eventually sue the government asking for an exemption from the CSA. The first of these churches is called União do Vegetal (UDV). This case began in the lower courts as *O Centro Espírita Beneficiente* v. *Ashcroft* (342 F.3d 1170, 2003) and progressed to the Supreme Court as *Gonzales* v. *União do Vegetal*.

The Supreme Court heard this case and issued a unanimous decision stating, first, that RFRA applied to federal laws, and second, that it protected the UDV's right to import ayahuasca (which it calls "hoasca"), to distribute it to members, and to consume it. We will return to the details of the UDV decision in Section 3, but for now we should note the decision's impact. In the wake of this decision, two branches of Santo Daime (another group that sacramentally consumes ayahuasca, which it calls "Daime") in Oregon sued for the right to import and consume ayahuasca. A district court in Oregon heard the case where the presiding judge applied the Supreme Court's decision in the UDV case to similarly conclude that the government needed to accommodate Santo Daime's importation and use of Daime (see Fernandes Antunes 2023). Collectively, these two cases empowered entheogenic users and activists who, for the first time, saw a potential legal rainbow in the otherwise dark legislative shadow cast by the CSA.

In the wake of these decisions, entheogenic activists and communities emerged from the underground or created new communities based upon the use of otherwise illegal psychoactive substances. Many of these communities and organizers ignored legal ramifications altogether. A growing number, however, wanted to embrace the courts' decisions and operate in the space these decisions hypothetically created. When the courts heard these two cases, the justices identified or articulated the factors that guided their judgments. These considerations, many entheogenic activists contend, provide instructions or a map of sorts for entheogenic communities to replicate if they, too, hope to someday win the legal right to consume their otherwise unlawful sacraments. This map, they soon found, requires conformity and replication. To understand how entheogenic attorneys address this map, we must first situate entheogenic churches within the larger context of the PR.

Set and Setting: Entheogenic Diversity in the Psychedelic Renaissance

As described earlier, the use of psychoactive substances predates colonialism by hundreds, or more likely, by thousands of years. The ceremonial and ritualistic use of these substances appears to have involved trained specialists who operated with the authority or approval of Indigenous political systems (Dawson 2018). Modern nation states replaced these governments, however, and developed their unique (and diverse) administrative and carceral procedures. For their part, some Native Americans reacted to these changes by creating the Native American Church, the first institutionalized organization that used the state's administrative and taxonomic structures to attempt to link religiosity with the use of peyote. As Marinacci (2023) and Lattin (2023) have documented, more Americans adopted this strategy in the wake of drug prohibition, when they completed the paperwork to receive state recognition as entheogenic communities that deserve the right to practice religious free-dom predicated on the use of otherwise illegal substances.

This strategy might have resulted in new churches, but these reformers never achieved their desired results of lobbying the state to allow them to be exempt from the generally applicable prohibition on drugs. Instead, many of the leaders and members of these communities were arrested, tried, and even incarcerated. These dynamics motivated some communities to close permanently, but some leaders and communities defied prohibition and continued to organize, meet, and consume otherwise illegal psychoactive substances.

In the twenty-first century, however, new waves of entheogenic leaders have felt empowered by the courts' decisions in the UDV and Santo Daime cases and created entheogenic communities in the wake of these decisions. These devel-opments overlapped with the broader resurging interest in psychedelics that defines the Psychedelic Renaissance (PR). These communities are important, particularly those that hire and consult attorneys to help them create new entheogenic churches that founders hope will resemble the courts' understand-ings of religiosity as expressed in various court cases.

Before we examine these attorneys and the entheogenic churches they help create, we must first recognize the diversity of entheogenic and psychedelic leaders and communities that exist today in the United States. This multiplicity is particularly hard to quantify, as many people in entheogenic and psychedelic spaces operate by word of mouth or advertise their services and ceremonies in private chat groups and in phone apps like Signal or WhatsApp. That is, they conceal their activities to various degrees, making it hard, or even impossible, to gauge the scope of their activities. The issue is further complicated by the fact that few entheogenic practitioners are willing to discuss their activities and beliefs with scholars. The discussion that follows, then, is an overview of the psychedelic landscape gathered from several years of ethnographic research that I have conducted; data gathered primarily through formal interviews, through participation in entheogenic ceremonies and events, and by observing the broader entheogenic ecosystem in social media and in private chat groups. This discussion is by no means comprehensive, but it does identify various models of psychedelic and entheogenic consumption.

To understand the variety of entheogenic and psychedelic leaders, communi-ties, and participants, we should first note that there are multiple paradigms for the consumption of psychedelics or entheogens. These different paradigms reflect the consumer's desire to choose the preferred "set" and "setting" (Hartogsohn 2017). Timothy Leary was not the first to use the terms set and setting, but he popularized the concepts in the early 1960s to highlight the ways that various factors influence psychedelic experiences, including the participant's mindset (set) and the environment (setting) in which they consume the substance (Pollan 2018a, 151). Each of these factors influences the experience and reflects the consumer's desire to achieve a particular outcome.

Someone consuming a psychedelic recreationally, for example, will have a different mindset or expectations than someone interested in having a spiritual or religious experience, as will someone who consumes these substances to achieve an outcome related to mental health. These outcomes and intentions are not mutually exclusive, as people routinely report that these results exist to some degree in most psychedelic experiences; however, the goal, the preparation, and the expectations are substantively different. The consumer's mindset or "set" largely determines the elements of the experience the person will focus on. Having identified a mindset for the consumption of a psychoactive substance, one then identifies the setting or environment in which they consume their psychoactive substance of choice.

One common setting involves a person choosing to have a solitary entheogenic experience. This person might have the experience in private, or they might consume the substance and go for a hike or walk in nature. In either event, the mindset is for a solitary religious or spiritual experience and the setting is a place of their choice where they can be alone or can be in a semipublic setting where they are not expected to interact with other people.

Entheogenic practitioners might also opt for a sitter. A sitter is someone who literally sits with the person and who cares for the person while they consume their substance of choice. David Hodges, founder of the Church of Ambrosia and Zide Door Church in Oakland and San Francisco, for example, is a champion of sitters (see Lattin 2023). To understand Hodges and his theories related to sitters, consider that Hodges believes that psychoactive mushrooms and cannabis are religious sacraments that occasion religious, spiritual, or mystical experiences. He also teaches what he calls the Religious Evolution doctrine, which contends that early humans first learned of "something more to our existence" by consuming psychoactive mushrooms (Hodges 2022). In other words, he believes that the consumption of psychedelic mushrooms first exposed people to "god" and occasioned the earliest religious experiences. To occasion these experiences today, Zide Door Church provides church members with these sacraments at its locations in Oakland and San Francisco. To that end, church members can enter the church during its open hours (seven days a week) and acquire psilocybin mushrooms and cannabis in exchange for a donation. Hodges estimates that upwards of 200 members per day acquire sacraments at the Oakland location alone.[10]

---

[10] Personal conversation with author, May 13, 2021.

In various public appearances, speeches, and interviews, Hodges has repeatedly discussed the importance of sitters (see, for example, Hodges 2022; De La Torre 2022). As he describes it, the sitter is tasked with helping the entheogenic practitioner with anything the person might need. Sitters might get or move blankets and pillows, they might fetch a glass of water, they might help clean up if the person purges in the form of vomit or diarrhea, and they otherwise monitor the person's safety. If the practitioner chose to consume the sacrament in nature, the sitter is also tasked with protecting the practitioner's physical body. Hodges told me, "Look, you can't be in another realm and have a bear come chewing on you or anything."[11] Hodges summarized the importance of sitters when he said, "I don't recommend anybody start this work without a sitter" (Hodges 2022).

Some people also claim to have entheogenic experiences in therapy, primarily related to ketamine-assisted therapy. Although it was first synthesized in 1962 on the eve of the counterculture or hippie movement, ketamine is not considered a "classic psychedelic" in the vein of LSD or psilocybin. It is, however, a dissociative anesthetic possessing what are often referred to as hallucinogenic properties. Ketamine is also a legal "Schedule III" drug (meaning, the government recognizes its medicinal value) and was subsequently introduced into clinical practice in the 1970s within the context of the growing war on drugs long before the PR.[12]

Within the context of the larger PR, however, ketamine-assisted psychotherapy (KAP) has grown exponentially, primarily used in the treatment of treatment-resistant depression and substance use disorders (see Joneborg et al. 2022). Some clinical providers offer KAP, and some formal ketamine clinics have opened as well. Some of the KAP providers operate under the assumption that ketamine is effective precisely because of its religious or spiritual (that is, entheogenic) properties. Courtney Watson is one such person who provides ketamine under the entheogenic paradigm.

Watson is a licensed marriage and family therapist, a certified sex therapist, the owner of Doorway Therapeutics Services, and the founder of a nonprofit called Access to Doorways.[13] Watson is also an African American woman who centers the treatment of members of BIPOC and LGBTQIA+ communities. When I interviewed Watson, she contended that while she's a supporter of psychedelic-assisted therapy (PAT) more broadly, she works with ketamine

---

[11] Personal conversation with author, May 13, 2021.

[12] For a summary of literature on ketamine before the PR, see Krupitsky and Grinenko 1997.

[13] Personal conversation with author, February 11, 2022. Access to Doorways is a nonprofit that subsidizes the cost of ketamine-assisted therapy for queer, BIPOC, and gender diverse people, as well as subsidizing the costs of training queer, BIPOC, and gender diverse therapists to learn how to perform psychedelic-assisted therapy.

because it is legal. She also discussed how ketamine is effective, not because it is a psychedelic, but because it possesses the "healing possibilities of entheogens." Watson elaborated when she said, "I take a spiritual perspective to this work. I don't think of ketamine as only a molecule; I think of her as a spirit. And I think that she has a healing spirit." Watson also explained that providers of PAT are an integral part of the PAT process, premised on their appreciation of the entheogenic nature of ketamine and psychedelics. For providers like Watson, if their clients will experience healing from ketamine or other psychedelics, this healing is the result of supernatural factors and experiences. From this logic, people have entheogenic experiences in what are otherwise deemed therapeutic environments.

Whether one has an entheogenic experience by themselves, under the supervision of a sitter, or in a therapeutic setting, the consumer of the psychoactive substance is typically journeying alone; meaning, that the consumer is the sole person under the influence of a psychedelic or entheogen. Someone who chooses to consume with a group, however, has various options for the group experience. Some people have extended groups of like-minded friends who meet informally to journey together. These people can meet in a home or gather in nature. In either case, there is no formal organization or group identity. Instead, these are just friends, acquaintances, or people "in the know" who meet to have a group experience.

Another option for people looking for a group format is to sit with a traveling facilitator who has no formal or stable community, but who works with people in various parts of the country to organize ceremonies when and where there is interest. Sometimes these traveling ceremony holders operate in the underground, but sometimes they advertise their services. Andrew Randall is one such person.[14]

Randall completed a shamanic training program in Peru and now offers ayahuasca and San Pedro ceremonies. Randall announces his offerings on his Instagram page and in a private Signal group, but despite his semipublic persona, he asked me not to disclose his real name. "I'm walking a fine line," he told me, "between putting myself out there so people can find me and not drawing attention to myself. I know that sounds contradictory, but yeah."[15] Randall's ceremonies are his sole source of income, and he estimates that he averages one retreat weekend per month, which means that he travels often. Groups of ten or more people contact Randall to arrange a customized retreat based on the group's desires. These retreats last as few as two nights, although

---

[14] At the facilitator's request, I assigned him a pseudonym.
[15] Personal conversation with author, November 11, 2021.

his longest was a ten-day retreat that included five ceremonies (three ayahuasca, two San Pedro).

Given his reputation and the positive responses from people who sit with him ("sitting" is a common term for participating in a ceremony while under the influence of a psychoactive substance), Randall contends that he could start a local community with people who repeatedly sit with him. He chooses to be a traveling facilitator, however, for several reasons. "The main reason," he told me, "is that I just love to travel. I also get exposed to new people everywhere I go. These people aren't always light and love, though, so it's also easier to walk away from someone when our energies aren't aligned." He later continued, "plus, I do have some people here that I hold space for a couple times a year, so I guess I have it both ways, so to speak." ("Holding space" is a common term that facilitators use to describe the ceremonial "space" they create, where a facilitator might sing, play music, or otherwise assist the person who consumes an entheogen.) Since Randall has a robust travel schedule and since he's importing illegal substances, flying domestically with them, and distributing them in multiple states, I asked Randall if he's worried about legal consequences of his actions and activities. "Not really," he said. "Like I said, I keep a low enough profile, and this is my religion, so, like, I don't want to be arrested, but if I am, I'll have a good defense" (Randall 2021).

As a traveling facilitator, Randall chose a model that few facilitators replicate. More common are local facilitators who don't have stable communities or formal churches, but who provide ceremonies close to their homes. Most of these facilitators have full- or part-time employment not related to psychedelics or entheogens, but they are contract facilitators who supplement their incomes by working in entheogenic spaces. A man named Kyle Connor is one such facilitator, who offers San Pedro ceremonies near his hometown of Philadelphia.[16] Unlike Randall, Connor does not advertise his ceremonies on social media. Instead, he operates by word-of-mouth referrals and he also advertises his ceremonies in various Signal groups that cater to the broader psychedelic community. Connor operates as a contract facilitator, meaning that he organizes group ceremonies without any expectation of forming a community after or outside the ceremony or of repeat clientele.

Connor told me that he chose the contract facilitator model for several specific reasons. The first is that his girlfriend and his day job keep him from traveling extensively, so he has no interest in being a traveling facilitator. Connor could create a formal church, but he indicated that the church model would require too much time and that he wants to minimize his exposure. He is

---

[16] At the facilitator's request, I assigned him a pseudonym.

open to someday forming a formal community of like-minded and recurring clients, but he doubts he'll ever be comfortable with creating a formal church. "This is totally a spiritual thing for me," he told me, "but I don't want to form a church and leave a paper trail telling the government that I'm holding San Pedro ceremonies. I do my thing, lay low, and people find me when they are ready. Plus, religion isn't really our thing. It's more spiritual than religious."[17] Connor continued to describe how he believes that churches are more formal, institutional, and impersonal; whereas, spirituality is more personal and informal, giving individuals more freedom to create their own truths and to connect with Source on their terms, not the group's. From this perspective, Connor is reluctant to create a church, as he believes that formal religion is a problem to be avoided, despite the potential legal safeguards it provides.

Qualitative ethnographic research suggests that the contract facilitator is the dominant model in entheogenic space. This is the primary type for various reasons, particularly those that Connor mentioned. Contract facilitators typically have full-time jobs and have personal relationships that keep them rooted in their local communities. These facilitators are typically active in their local psychedelic ecosystems, which supply them with ample access to interested clients. Contract facilitators control the frequency of their offerings and typically are not beholden to congregations or to any group. This independence allows them maximum flexibility with minimum accountability. Contract facilitators do what they want, when they want, and with whom they want. They typically charge several hundred dollars per person for their ceremonies, which provide potentially lucrative supplemental incomes. Contract facilitators usually have low start-up costs, the most common being the training that one needs to facilitate the ceremony and the expenses to acquire the substance being consumed. This training can be expensive, especially if someone has to travel abroad to complete it, but there are also online certifications and various self-styled shamanic institutes that offer specific training.[18]

Contract facilitators are also prevalent because there are many substances and ceremonial offerings that they can host or provide. These include ayahuasca,

---

[17] Personal conversation with author, March 18, 2021.

[18] The issue of training is particularly important for people who serve ayahuasca, peyote, or kambo (kambo is secreted by a specific frog and is commonly administered for medicinal purposes [see Sacco et al. 2022]). All three of these substances have been used by Indigenous people prior to colonialism, and all three can be deadly if the wrong person consumes them, so training programs typically involve extensive overviews of safety protocols. Ayahuasca and peyote specifically are associated with opening supernatural realms, so potential facilitators are typically taught to be familiar with these realms and with the range of entities that people commonly claim to encounter. One can only become familiar with these realms and entities by using the substances extensively, so facilitators in Indigenous communities generally train for years. In recent decades, training centers have formed in South American countries like Peru and Brazil,

peyote, San Pedro, MDMA, DMT, and 5-MeO-DMT (a psychoactive trypta-mine found in some plants and secreted by the Colorado river toad; see Oroc 2009). This diversity of ceremonial offerings and services makes it comparably easy to enter the profession, especially as an adjunct to a full- or part-time job.

Some contract facilitators provide ceremonies and services that are entirely legal.[19] Cacao ceremonies, for example, are legal in all fifty states, where people gather to ceremonially consume chocolate beverages. People who facilitate these and other ceremonies run their businesses like any other legal entity or enterprise. Contract facilitators who serve illicit psychoactive substances, how-ever, are more at risk, as the courts have yet to formally approve the legality of a contract facilitator. I have interviewed several dozen contract facilitators, and despite these risks, very few of them are worried about the legal implications of their work. Like Connor, they believe they are protected by religious freedom laws, although very few are versed in these laws. One such facilitator summa-rized the dominant attitude when she said

> I mean, what I'm doing is spiritual. It is religious. We have the First Amendment, right? The Constitution says everyone is entitled to religious freedom, so I'm protected. I might someday have to fight that battle in court, but gods willing, I'll win, and I'll win because of the Constitution.[20]

Contract facilitators typically have repeat clientele, and sometimes these clients may be informal groups of like-minded psychonauts (the common term for psychedelic journeyers; see Jay 2023). These groups are not organized churches and lack stable or formal membership. Instead, they are typically friends, acquaintances, or people who share a collective interest in psychedelics or entheogens and who choose to repeatedly sit in ceremony together. I am aware of roughly a half-dozen of these groups (commonly called a circle or a tribe) that operate near my home in Baltimore. One is a group of about thirty

---

which offer shorter training protocols that begin with one month of training. Qualitative research demonstrates that many entheogenic practitioners are skeptical of people who complete these comparably short trainings, whom they disparagingly term "plastic shamans" (Aldred 2000; Arregi 2021). Ayahuasca is also associated with shamanic healing, where the facilitator is believed to enter the spirit world with the participant and to be an agent facilitating healing. These facilitators acquire these powers both by sitting with ayahuasca extensively and by completing "plant dietas" (Beyer 2009). Plant dietas are based on the idea that specific plants in the Amazon and beyond are associated with supernatural powers. By repeatedly consuming a drink commonly made by soaking the tree's bark or the plant itself in water, the facilitator is thought to acquire the plant or tree's healing powers. The facilitator is then able to harness the power for the sake of healing the participant. People often sit with plant dietas for several years.

[19] Kambo, hapeh, mushrooms, cacao, meditation, reiki, divination, yoga, and various forms of sound healing are some of the more common licit services, ceremonies, and classes that contract facilitators offer.

[20] Personal conversation with author, Sept. 18, 2021. At the facilitator's request, I assigned her a pseudonym.

people who have no official leader or administrative structure, but who sit together in ceremony multiple times each year. Another is a group of professionals primarily in their fifties or older who meet at one of the members' houses in Baltimore County, a rural area where no one would suspect that white, middle-aged, affluent professionals are meeting to consume psychedelics or entheogens. Neither of these groups has a preferred sacrament. Instead, they hire contract facilitators, partner with a local provider to facilitate a ceremony, or simply offer the substance to attendees absent the oversight of a sitter or facilitator. One month the substance might be psilocybin, the next it might be MDMA, and the next it might be a combination of legal and illegal substances. These groups announce the ceremony and invite interested parties to attend. People register in advance and attend the ceremony at the agreed-upon time. Preliminary ethnographic research suggests that circles or tribes of this nature exist across the country and are growing rapidly.

Finally, in addition to sitters, informal groups, traveling facilitators, contract facilitators, and mental health providers, formal entheogenic communities and churches exist in the United States and their numbers are growing. These churches have completed requisite paperwork with the state and federal governments registering them as official religious institutions. Many of these churches are single-sacrament communities, meaning that they only sanction and facilitate the consumption of a particular substance, but other churches are multisacrament. Despite this difference, many of these churches typically share several factors in common. First, they hire experienced attorneys who specialize in creating entheogenic communities. These attorneys interpret existing law and help create churches that exist within their interpretations of the confines of these laws. Second, these churches tend to do more than simply hold ceremonies. They also hold integration sessions where people can discuss their successes and frustrations as they try to implement changes based on ceremonial experiences and insights. They hold weekly or regularly scheduled discussions or presentations ("sermons," of sorts), or they hold community events like potlucks and book clubs. They also host or organize additional ceremonies for events like changes in the lunar calendar or meditation classes.

These churches typically hide in plain sight, so to speak, where they operate like other churches. That is, they have websites, social media accounts, and newsletters that advertise their various ceremonies and community events. These churches are important because they represent the most recent manifestation of groups that assert religious freedom claims to advocate for their right to exist and to consume otherwise illegal psychoactive substances. As we will see in the next section, they contend that existing law justifies their existence, and for the most part, they are willing to exist within the boundaries of their interpretations of the law.

Collectively, this analysis suggests that there is a diversity of entheogenic practitioners and that these practitioners provide their services in various formats and settings. When someone decides to hold space for people, they face the inevitable choice of identifying a model to embrace. We have already identified several factors that influence this decision; however, no discussion of entheogenic providers would be complete that does not address the issue of intersectionality (Crenshaw 1989), and more specifically, race.

Race, ethnicity, and Indigeneity are particularly important in the entheogenic ecosystem because, among other reasons, most facilitators in the United States are white. They are serving psychoactive substances that Indigenous communities have used for hundreds, if not thousands, of years. Moreover, white colonizers repeatedly and on multiple continents persecuted the users of these substances. Today, however, white facilitators hold ceremonies and typically charge attendees hundreds if not thousands of dollars (Lucia 2020). These facilitators are particularly controversial, and Indigenous people and their allies often refer to white facilitators as plastic shamans, or people who lack the extensive training associated with Indigenous use of these substances, and as people who engage in cultural appropriation (Hobson 2002).

Some facilitators, however, are African Americans, Native Americans, and other people of color. Like all active facilitators, these individuals have to choose a model of entheogenic provider, and ethnographic research suggests that the issue of race is always a factor that impacts their actions and organizations. Consider that contract facilitators, tripsitters, or informal communities typically operate in the underground, where they maintain a higher degree of anonymity. This anonymity carries its own risks, however, as the courts have not sanctioned or affirmed the legality of these providers. Churches, on the other hand, are formal institutions that – by virtue of filing the paperwork to receive state or government recognition as a church – are more public than informal groups, contract facilitators, and tripsitters. As I will discuss in detail later in this Element, entheogenic attorneys increasingly contend that the church model of entheogenic activity is, legally speaking, the safest model.

BIPOC entheogenic providers have various reactions to these dynamics. Tyrell Henderson, an African American entheogenic activist in Oakland, California, described his aversion to the church model when he told me that "racist America has a history of limiting and directing black people, so I just ain't gonna play. Tell me to form a church? I ain't forming no church."[21]

---

[21] Personal conversation with author, April 24, 2022. At the person's request, I assigned him a pseudonym.

Instead, Henderson sits in informal circles. He is aware that his activities are legally tenuous, but he also told me, "being black is the problem. It's not the sacraments. If they're gonna get me, it's because I'm black – not because I sit with mushrooms." Based on the ethnographic interviews I conducted, I found that Henderson described a common sentiment when he expressed his desire to follow his own path as a form of resistance. Another African American entheogenic consumer has a similar, but different perspective on the issue.

Ayize Jama-Everett is an important figure in entheogenic circles in and near Oakland, California.[22] In addition to writing science fiction novels, Jama-Everett is an entheogenic activist and consumer, an educator, and writer and director of *A Table of Our Own*, a documentary about BIPOC entheogenic practitioners. Many people in his broader community consider him an elder whom they approach for wisdom and insights. He is also a founding member of an entheogenic church he subsequently left and, in 2023, is currently contemplating creating another formal church, albeit one more narrowly focused on serving the needs of the BIPOC community. This focus has Jama-Everett envisioning the model of entheogenic community he will help create, as he fears that the church model will not provide him and other people of color the same degree of protection that it provides for white church founders. "In general," he told me, "I don't think a lot of black people are like, 'Oh, don't worry, we filed this paperwork, we're good with the state, the feds recognize us, and so we're gonna be okay.'" With this in mind, Jama-Everett is reluctant to create a formal church, which leaves a paper trail and an official record of some aspects of his community.

While Jama-Everett is hesitant about starting a church for his BIPOC community, some BIPOC facilitators do form churches, but they limit the services they provide. The founders of Temple Pachamama offer a clear example.[23] Located in a major American city, Temple Pachamama is a thriving community founded by a African American couple. It caters predominantly to the BIPOC community. According to the founders, ideally, Temple Pachamama would be a multisacrament church. Due to their race, however, they largely limit their offerings to substances that are legal, particularly kambo, a secretion from an Amazonian tree frog long used as a healing purgative. Kambo is legal in the United States, so Temple Pachamama publicly advertises that it offers this sacrament. In the rare event when the Temple offers a sacrament that is otherwise illegal, however, the group limits its marketing to people in their inner circle. In other words, the founders of Temple Pachamama, like

---

[22] Personal conversation with author, January 30, 2024.
[23] At the founders' request, this is a fictitious name designed to protect their anonymity.

the other African American providers discussed in this Element, are aware of the additional burdens they face as people of color. They respond differently to these burdens, but these burdens do impact their behaviors and communities.

In short, this Element demonstrates that entheogenic practitioners and providers have various options or models for providing entheogenic sacraments. These models carry various degrees of exposure and liabilities, depending on a combination of diverse factors. Entheogenic attorneys typically contend that, legally speaking, the church model is safest, provided that the founders of these churches create institutions and present religiosity in terms recognizable to the courts as such. The next section in this Element discusses in detail the legal counsel that these attorneys provide.

3 Entheogenic Attorneys and the Evolving Entheogenic Ecosystem

In the twenty-first century, lawyers interested in the psychedelic ecosystem have more career opportunities than ever before. Companies like Atai Life Sciences and Compass Pathways, for example, are investing hundreds of millions of dollars into psychedelic research (see Jesse Lee 2023). In addition to the various legal considerations that every business must contend with, these companies bear the additional burden of navigating the complex legal worlds surrounding psychedelic research. Thus, large companies like these typically employ attorneys who are both business specialists and experts in the growing field of psychedelic law. Corporations, however, are not the only ones researching psychedelics. Scholars in various universities and nonprofit organizations, like the Multidisciplinary Association for Psychedelic Studies (MAPS), are also conducting psychedelic research, and these organizations similarly employ in-house attorneys who specialize in psychedelic law.

In addition to the attorneys working for companies or nonprofits in the larger psychedelic ecosystem, some attorneys are increasingly focusing on entheogenic law and are providing legal counsel to entheogenic communities. Attorney Gary Smith, for example, fashions himself an expert on contracting and construction law in Arizona (Smith 2020).[24] He is also a member of the Peyote Way Church of God and its general legal counsel. Smith is an expert on cannabis law as well, and he occasionally offers legal counsel to other entheogenic communities. Smith is but one lawyer who offers this type of counsel.

In the otherwise growing field of entheogenic law, several attorneys have gained nationwide reputations and work with people across the country to form entheogenic churches. By almost any metric, attorneys Greg Lake and Ian

---

[24] Personal conversation with Author, September 18, 2020.

Benouis are among the more influential attorneys in this corner of the entheogenic ecosystem. From a certain perspective, Lake and Benouis might appear to have complicated relationships with the psychoactive substances they call entheogens or sacred plant medicines. Greg Lake's experience with drugs began at age twelve, when he consumed his first tab of LSD.[25] He continued to use and be addicted to drugs and alcohol for seventeen years, and in 2011, he first consumed psilocybin mushrooms. Lake subsequently completed law school and practiced law for three years as an addict, but he ultimately became sober during a thirty-two-month stint in a therapeutic facility. After his release in 2018, he returned to mushrooms, this time as a means of spiritual and religious discovery and to help overcome the sometimes intense anxiety associated with his recovery. He continued to practice law in Louisiana, specializing in maritime law, but his personal experience with entheogens motivated him to study the evolving field of entheogenic law.

Ian Benouis is a West Point graduate and former Army officer who flew Black Hawk helicopters in the US invasion of Panama in 1989–1990.[26] Like many people before him and after, Benouis emerged from combat with PTSD, a condition he managed with various psychoactive plant medicines like ayahuasca and 5-MeO-DMT. After a brief career as a pharmaceutical representative, Benouis graduated from law school and became an attorney in Texas, focusing on intellectual property. His love and respect for entheogens, however, motivated him to increasingly focus on entheogenic law.

Lake and Benouis met and bonded over their shared interest in entheogens and entheogenic-assisted healing. Today, they are among the nation's leading entheogenic attorneys who have helped hundreds of people draft and file the paperwork to create entheogenic churches. They have appeared on numerous podcasts and have presented papers and delivered speeches and presentations at conferences across the country. Lake also created Entheoconnect, which he describes as "a worldwide social media platform for those in the entheogen/ spirituality community, as well as ceremony and retreat listings in the US and abroad" (Lake 2021, v). The two men also started their own entheogenic church, the Church of Psilomethoxin, later renamed the Church of the Sacred Synthesis, a community that consumes psychoactive mushrooms.[27]

---

[25] Personal conversation with author, November 20, 2022.

[26] Personal conversation with author, November 21, 2022.

[27] Lake and Benouis formed this church in 2022 and it was quickly embroiled in controversy. They claimed that the church's sacrament was a novel tryptamine, or a new psychedelic. As scholars Samuel Williamson and Alexander Sherwood describe the church, "The Church of Psilomethoxin claims to produce a novel tryptamine by adding 5-MeO-DMT to the substrate of cultivated Psilocybe mushrooms, which is then biosynthesized into psilomethoxin, the church's sacrament" (Williamson & Sherwood 2023, unnumbered page). People across the

In addition to these various projects and to the larger contributions they have made to the psychedelic ecosystem, Lake is particularly important because he has self-published three books on psychedelics, including two books that specifically address the law, titled *The Law of Entheogenic Churches in the United States,* volumes one and two. These books are particularly important because they summarize in detail the theories and interpretations of US law and court precedent that underlie Lake's legal advice and counsel. In other words, Lake and Benouis are helping usher in a new era of entheogenic churches, and these two volumes summarize the legal advice that the two attorneys provide to their clients.

As described in these books and in their various public talks and presentations, Lake and Benouis believe that entheogens should be legal and available for anyone who wants to consume them medicinally or sacramentally. They recognize, however, that entheogens are still illegal, so in *The Law of Entheogenic Churches in the United States*, vol. 1 (2021), Lake attempted to summarize and to interpret existing laws that either directly or indirectly relate to entheogenic communities. Based on the sum of his legal analysis, Lake then offered a "General Guide to forming a non-profit Church" and concluded by responding to frequently asked questions. Lake repeats some of this material in the second volume (2022), where he also summarized the broader history of entheogenic drug use and where he analyzed a specific ayahuasca church's struggles with the Drug Enforcement Agency (DEA).

Collectively, these two volumes remind the reader that Lake is first and foremost an entheogenic activist and advocate. He unequivocally stated as much when he wrote,

> I decided that I would dedicate my life to the widespread legalization and acceptance of entheogens across the world. Seeing the mass decay in mental and spiritual health around the world, I knew these substances could provide the relief that many seek but never find through traditional western medicine. (Lake 2021, v)

---

country joined the church by submitting an online application and were granted access to the church's sacrament, which they received via mail. The so-called "mail-order mushroom church" attracted a lot of attention; but the church received even more scrutiny and condemnation after Williamson and Sherwood conducted tests on the church's sacrament and were not able to find evidence of psilomethoxin. They did, however, find psilocybin, baeocystin, and psilocin, suggesting the church was distributing and consuming "normal" psychedelic mushrooms. They published their results in April 2023 and subsequently amended their findings in June 2023. The findings were quite damning, putting Lake and Benouis on the defensive and ultimately prompting them to change the church's name to Church of the Sacred Synthesis. Lake himself responded publicly to the controversy on the Plus Three podcast in May 2023 (Lake 2023).

In addition to, and as an extension of, his activism, Lake is also an attorney who seeks to understand the law so he can help his clients navigate and apply it. As we saw in the discussion of the various types of psychedelic settings, circles, and ceremonies, not everyone in psychedelic or entheogenic space is interested in creating formal churches.

Attorneys like Lake, however, try to understand the law so they can operate, to the extent that they can, within its parameters. Lake recognizes that there are multiple models of entheogenic communities, and he advises his clients to curtail some of their activities and formats for the sake of modeling themselves after the few entheogenic communities that have received state-approved exemptions to consume their sacraments. He contends that his writings do not constitute legal advice or counsel, but they do reflect his opinion. "I would like to note my opinion," he wrote, "that a sacred ceremony involving entheogens, consummated in a manner that places safety and substance handling as a priority, is generally a protected activity under the federal RFRA" (Lake 2021, 65). He continues to state that it is his legal opinion that if the government initiates legal actions against an entheogenic leader or community, that leader or community has a stronger case under RFRA if they replicate the structures and beliefs that the courts have previously approved. Lake said as much when he wrote:

> There is no blanket protection for the sacramental use of entheogenic sacra-
> ments. However, as we examine the precedent on this issue, we will be able to
> discern which facts are important to the courts in deciding these cases. This in
> turn helps inform us on how to structure entheogenic churches, ceremonies,
> and retreats in a manner most likely to be protected by the courts under the
> federal and state RFRA statutes. (Lake 2021, 11)

In other words, the goal is to replicate instead of innovate.

Identifying Religious Sincerity

Lake began *The Law of Entheogenic Churches in the United States* by acknowl-
edging that, as demonstrated by two important court cases involving a psychoactive tea referred to by many names (most commonly ayahuasca), RFRA is the standard that courts will use to adjudicate cases related to entheo-
genic communities. Before he addressed these two cases, however, Lake first wanted to "examine what constitutes a 'religious' practice or exercise under the RFRA" (Lake 2021, 13). The problem is that while RFRA's congressional authors wanted to issue a broad endorsement of religious freedom, RFRA does not define religion, nor does it offer standards or guidelines for courts to use when they attempt to identify religion, religiosity, or religious sincerity.

Lake acknowledged the resulting ambiguity when he asked, "What constitutes sincerity in the context of a RFRA claim? Unfortunately, there is no 'bright line' test to determine whether a religious belief is sincerely held" (Lake 2021, 13). In other words, he acknowledged that there is no common sincerity test and that there is no single factor that determines a group's religiosity or religious sincerity, nor is there a standard or legally binding list of requirements that courts will use to determine religiosity or religious sincerity. Lake then quoted the Fifth Circuit Court, which acknowledged the problems courts encounter when they attempt to assess religious sincerity. The issue, the court wrote, "must be handled with a light touch, or 'judicial shyness'" (compare Lake 2021, 14).

If Lake belabors the issue, it is precisely because he acknowledges that the issue of religious sincerity is the primary question in entheogenic communities, as RFRA only purports to protect religious behavior. Casual or recreational drug users lack standing under RFRA, and Lake acknowledged that entheogenic practitioners will most likely have to convince the courts of their religiosity. These factors, combined with RFRA's protection of the sincerely held religiosity that it does not define, motivated Lake to identify and describe in detail the various approaches the courts have used to identify religious sincerity.

To this end, Lake summarized two approaches the courts have taken to recognizing religion and to determining religious sincerity. The first approach appears in the case *United States* v. *Meyers* (906 F.Supp 1494 [D. Wyo. 1995]), where, according to Lake, "the district court conducted an exhaustive review of prior case law in order to create a list of the relevant factors that have been considered by courts throughout the years in determining what constitutes a 'religion'" (Lake 2021, 15). The court compiled this list because it had to determine the religiosity of someone charged with trafficking marijuana. The defendant, David Meyers, rejected this allegation, claiming that he was the reverend of the Church of Marijuana. The court responded to this assertion by acknowledging that Meyers' potential religiosity was a "delicate issue" (*Meyers*, 1495) that, if determined to be authentically religious, would trigger RFRA. Tasked, then, with assessing Meyers' religiosity, the court attempted to create "The Definition of 'Religion' under RFRA" (*Meyers*, 1498).

To that end, the justices acknowledged that the courts are tasked with protecting the "indefinable." They then attempted to have it both ways when they wrote,

> this Court has canvassed the cases on religion and catalogued the many factors that the courts have used to determine whether a set of beliefs is "religious" for First Amendment purposes. These factors, as listed below, impose some structure on the word "religion." (*Meyers*, 1501)

The court created a list of factors that can assist judges in determining religiosity, even as it stated that no single or combination of factors was necessary and sufficient to determine religiosity or religious sincerity. This list would become important to Lake, who bases some of his legal counsel on these factors.

As Lake discusses at length in his book, the court concluded in *Meyers* that religions commonly address or concern ultimate ideas, metaphysical beliefs, and moral or ethical systems. Another aspect of religion is "comprehensiveness of beliefs," meaning, that "More often than not, such beliefs provide a telos, an overarching array of beliefs that coalesce to provide the believer with answers to many, if not most, of the problems and concerns that confront humans. In other words, religious beliefs generally are not confined to one question or a single teaching" (*Meyers*, 1502). Finally, the court also concluded that religions commonly contain ten "accoutrements," including founder, prophet, or teacher; important writings; gathering places; keepers of knowledge; ceremonies and rituals; structure or organization; holidays; diet or fasting; appearance and clothing; and propagation (*Meyers*, 1502–3). The court emphasized that these accoutrements should serve as more of a guide than a list of comprehensive requirements when it wrote, "the Court again emphasizes that no one of these factors is dispositive, and that the factors should be seen as criteria that, if minimally satisfied, counsel the inclusion of beliefs within the term 'religion'" (*Meyers*, 1503).

If the *Meyers* case provides Lake with one set of criteria the courts might use to adjudicate religiosity and religious sincerity, the attorney also describes what he calls the "functional approach" (Lake 2021, 22) to determining religious sincerity. To explore the functional approach, Lake cites the court's opinion in the case *United States* v. *Hoffman* (2020), where the court analyzed "whether the beliefs professed . . . are sincerely held and whether they are in [a claimant's] own scheme of things, religious. . . . 'Religious' beliefs, then, are those that stem from a person's 'moral, ethical, or religious beliefs about what is right and wrong' and are 'held with the strength of traditional religious convictions'" (cf. Lake 2021, 22–3). Lake then highlighted how this approach does not attempt to define religion or to evaluate it in relation to its various components; rather, "it looks to whether a set of beliefs serves the same function as traditional religion in an individual's life" (Lake 2021, 22–3).

The functional approach will become important to Lake, who cited the case *United States* v. *Lepp*, where the Ninth Circuit Court "discarded" the *Meyers* approach in favor of the functional approach (Lake 2021, 23). This abandonment elevates the importance of the functional approach to determining if a set of beliefs is religious and if these beliefs are sincerely held, but Lake writes comparably little about it. Instead, in three paragraphs, he contends that this belief-centered approach is preferable to the criteria outlined in the *Meyers* case, as "that what might not qualify as religious under the *Meyers* factors, could qualify under the functional approach" (Lake 2021, 23). Lake did not elaborate further on the significance of the functional approach specifically as it relates to entheogenic communities, although he returned to the issue later in his book.

Applying RFRA to Sincerely Held Entheogenic Religion

Having addressed several ways the courts might evaluate someone's religiosity, Lake continued with his analysis of RFRA. Lake addressed the first element of RFRA when he attempted to identify how the courts might determine whether the enforcement of a law imposes a substantial burden on the exercise of religion. He has comparably little to say on this topic, simply noting that the Supreme Court has determined that laws create a "substantial burden" on religion when they place "substantial pressure on [a religious] adherent to modify his behavior and to violate his beliefs" (see Lake 2021, 24). Based on this analysis, Lake then concluded that "In the context of entheogenic churches and religions, this standard should always be met" (Lake 2021, 24). Since entheogenic ceremonies are contingent on the use of otherwise illegal psychoactive substances, these communities should have little trouble demonstrating that prohibition imposes a substantial burden on their religiosity, as it prevents them from holding ceremonies and presumably from having the religious experiences that are central to their religiosity itself. This, Lake contended, clearly addresses the applicability of RFRA's first prong to entheogenic communities.

RFRA's second prong states that the government can only substantially burden a person's exercise of religion if there is a compelling governmental interest. The third prong states that if such an interest exists, then the government must take the least restrictive means of substantially burdening religion. To explore these prongs and their applicability to entheogenic communities, Lake examined two important court cases involving ayahuasca, where the courts applied RFRA to assess two groups' abilities to import, distribute to members, and consume ayahuasca.

The first and most important of these cases is *O Centro Espírita Beneficiente União Do Vegetal* v. *Ashcroft* (342 F.3d 1170, 2003), a case decided by the Court of Appeals for the Tenth Circuit. The US District Court for the District of New Mexico first heard this case in 2002, where it ruled in favor of the UDV (282 F. Supp. 2d 1271). The following year, the case was relitigated by the Tenth Circuit before it subsequently went to the Supreme Court in the form of *Gonzales* v. *O Centro Espírita Beneficente União do Vegetal* (UDV; 546 US 418, 2006). In other words, three separate courts heard this case. Lake discussed the Tenth Circuit case at length, although readers should note that the attorney occasionally referenced the earlier District Court's case. Lake explained why he focused his discussion on the Tenth Circuit court's decision instead of the Supreme Court's decision when he wrote that "it provides the most information regarding the 'meat and potatoes' of the court's analysis under RFRA" (Lake 2021, 25–26). In other words, Lake concentrated on this case because it addressed the issues the Supreme Court would later consider, where the court would endorse the circuit court's decision.

The second case is *Church of Holy Light and Queen* v. *Mukasey* (615 F. Supp.2d 1210 1, 2009), a case decided in a district court in Oregon, where the presiding judge applied the Supreme Court's decision in *Gonzales* v. *UDV*. These two cases both concern ayahuasca and two separate ayahuasca communities in the United States. To understand the significance of these cases, especially as they pertain to laws involving groups that want to be recognized as religions, it is necessary to explore the history of ayahuasca itself and the formation of the two communities that are the subjects of these cases. Readers will note, first, that ayahuasca is traditionally consumed in the Amazon; second, that Indigenous people in the Amazon have a diversity of models for consuming ayahuasca; and third, that none of them resemble the church-based models of ayahuasca consumption growing in the United States.

Ayahuasca, Hoasca, Daime . . . The Sacrament with Many Names

The term "ayahuasca" is the Hispanicized spelling of a word in the Quechuan family of languages, which is commonly translated as "vine of the soul" (Beyer 2009, 207). In common usage, the term ayahuasca references a psychoactive drink derived from various plants indigenous to the Amazon. The most common recipes involve the ayahuasca vine (*banisteriopsis caapi*) and chacruna (*psychotria viridis*) leaves, which are subsequently boiled for upwards of twenty hours. These two ingredients are important because they work in tandem to create or occasion the psychoactive experience associated with ayahuasca. For their part, chacruna leaves supply DMT, an organic and naturally occurring tryptamine that exists in many plants and animals (Strassman 2001). When consumed properly, DMT can produce or occasion what is commonly described as a psychedelic or entheogenic experience. This is where the ayahuasca vine becomes important, as it contains reversible monoamine oxidase inhibitors (MAOIs), which allow the body to absorb the DMT when consumed orally. Chacruna can be substituted for other DMT-rich plants, and brewers can add adjuncts during the brewing process, with plants like ayahuma or mapacho among the more common (Labate et al. 2010).

There are multiple ways to prepare the various drinks that are commonly called ayahuasca, and different communities have different names for their respective brews. In other words, the term ayahuasca encompasses possibly an infinite number of recipes, which change from preparer to preparer and often from brew to brew. Additionally, practitioners claim that both the method of preparation and the ingredients themselves can change the final product, resulting in distinct brews that deserve unique names (Beyer 2009; Dawson 2013).

In any case, some Indigenous people in the Amazon have consumed ayahuasca for thousands of years. It is highly unlikely that we will ever reliably reconstruct the history of ayahuasca, but scientists have confirmed the presence of ayahuasca in hair samples that date back roughly 2,000 years ago (Nalewicki 2022), and archeologists confirmed the presence of ayahuasca in a small pouch that is roughly 1,000 years old (Miller et al. 2019). As these suggest, the use of ayahuasca predates the colonial era by hundreds if not thousands of years.

People who drink ayahuasca commonly describe the experience by referencing two overlapping themes or paradigms. The first is the healing or medical paradigm, as people who consume ayahuasca routinely claim to experience physical and psychological healing (Labate & Cavnar 2021). The health or medical paradigm is particularly and increasingly appealing to Americans and to the burgeoning emphasis on mental health. This approach is driving thousands of Americans annually to ayahuasca retreats in South America (Fotiou 2010) and to ayahuasca churches in the United States. The lure of potential medical and mental health benefits is also increasingly the subject of academic research (see, for example, Hamill et al. 2019; Jiménez-Garrido et al. 2020).

In addition to the medical model, people routinely use the language of religion and spirituality to describe ayahuasca experiences. When someone drinks ayahuasca, they typically lie down and wait roughly thirty minutes to an hour before they begin to experience the effects. Over the next five to six hours, people often report direct encounters with the supernatural. Each person's journey is different, but people frequently report experiencing a kaleidoscopic show of lights and images, traveling to different realms of existence, encountering and interacting with entities or beings, acquiring sacred knowledge about the nature of existence, and undergoing ego death and being absorbed by or becoming one with "Source."[28] Because ayahuasca is so

---

[28] Many of the people in the broader entheogenic ecosystems today have a complicated relationship with the word god, so they instead often refer to Creator or Source. Many entheogenic consumers believe the word god is too laden with Christian associations (particularly associations with conservative Christianity), so they refrain from using the word to highlight the various ways that "Source" is distinct from Christian notions of deity. Not all people who consume entheogens

intimately associated with the supernatural, Indigenous peoples in the Amazon have long consumed it to consult the supernatural and to have direct interactions with it.

Scholars have described various ways that groups or individuals have consumed ayahuasca. In some instances, the ayahuascero or curandero either drinks the ayahuasca for the purpose of healing someone or they drink ayahuasca with the person who needs healing (see Beyer 2009). The former is the person responsible for preparing and serving the ayahuasca, commonly called "shaman" by most entheogenic practitioners today and by Indigenous ayahuasceros or curanderos who cater to ayahuasca tourists (see Stoddard 2024). In other instances, it appears as though men are allowed to drink the ayahuasca with the ayahuascero or curandero, and women are allowed to consume ayahuasca when they are not menstruating. All these ceremonies, however, are ad hoc, so to speak, and they occur outside the confines of the institutional structures or "churches" that are usually associated with religiosity in the United States.

During the colonial period, knowledge of ayahuasca remained largely confined to the Indigenous peoples who lived in the jungle, where some continued to harvest, manufacture, and drink it. That began to change in the 1900s, with the formation of three groups that tend to highlight their differences but share much in common. Two of these groups, União do Vegetal and Santo Daime, are particularly important for this Element. They both originated in Brazil; they blend Catholic Christianity with the consumption of ayahuasca; and the founders of the respective groups were mestizo rubber tappers who entered the jungle to work, who consumed ayahuasca, and who brought knowledge of this practice outside the jungle and into Brazilian cities (Dawson 2013; Barnard 2022). Both groups arrived in North America around the year 1990 and both had legal encounters in the United States that collectively altered the religious freedom laws that are inspiring legions of Americans to create entheogenic communities in the twenty-first century.

The first of these groups is called Santo Daime, an organization founded in 1930 in Rio Branco, Brazil, by Raimundo Irineu Serra (1890–1971), who learned of ayahuasca while working as a rubber tapper in the jungle. As anthropologist Andrew Dawson reported, there are several versions of Serra's first interactions with ayahuasca (Dawson 2013, 10–11), but the dominant version of his earliest experience with ayahuasca is that a woman appeared to him calling herself the "Universal Goddess" or "Queen of the Forest," a figure that Serra associated with the Virgin Mary. As independent scholar Stephan

---

share this concern, including some Native Americans and other Indigenous peoples, in addition to white Americans like Rev. Hunt Priest, a Christian minister who consumed psilocybin mushrooms and who created Ligare, a Christian psychedelic society (Priest 2022).

Beyer wrote, "She told him that ayahuasca was the sacred blood of Jesus Christ, giving light, love, and strength to all who would use it. Ayahuasca was henceforth to be called *daime*, 'give me,' as in 'give me love, give me light, give me strength'" (Beyer 2009, 289). Based on this insight and on his desire to bring healing to his people, in the late 1920s Serra held his first ceremonies and began building his community.

Serra led the small but growing Santo Daime community as it expanded into larger Brazilian cities. As it spread, it caught the attention of people outside Brazil, including a young American acupuncturist named Jonathan Goldman. In 1987, Goldman accompanied his therapist to Brazil thinking that he could "do the equivalent of 10 years of psychotherapy and 10 years of meditation in a month."[29] Goldman ultimately became an initiate in the Brazilian Santo Daime community and in 1993, began holding small ceremonies in the United States. In October 1996, he officially opened the church in Oregon according to the protocols of the Santo Daime Path.

While Goldman was busy creating a Santo Daime community, Jeffrey Bronfman simultaneously and independently built a similar community in New Mexico rooted in the União do Vegetal (UDV) tradition (Beyer 2009). The UDV was created in Brazil by another rubber tapper, José Gabriel da Costa (1922–1971). Like Serra, da Costa first consumed ayahuasca while working in the jungle near the Bolivian border. He formed the UDV in 1961, which considers itself a Christian Spiritist religion premised on the sacramental consumption of ayahuasca – which the community calls hoasca or vegetal – and on following Jesus's teachings. Da Costa led the community until his death in 1971, when the group assumed its current name, Centro Espírita Beneficente União do Vegetal (Beyer 2009, 291). The community subsequently expanded, and according to the organization itself, is practiced by more than 21,000 people organized into communities (or núcleos) in eleven countries (https://udvusa.org/).

The UDV eventually contacted an environmental organization in the United States to seek help with a conservation project. The group was growing and harvesting the raw ingredients they subsequently use to create hoasca, so they solicited the help of philanthropist Jeffrey Bronfman, one of the heirs to the Seagram's liquor fortune. Bronfman "had been working for a number of years with a private foundation that did funding in the area of environmental conservation and the preservation of tribal cultural traditions" (Dobkin de Rios & Grob 2005). He received the UDV's proposal and subsequently traveled to Brazil, where he interacted with the group, consumed hoasca, and became a convert and official group member. The UDV has a reputation for being a very

---

[29] Personal conversation with author, December 21, 2021.

hierarchical organization (Beyer 2009), and Bronfman eventually received permission to create a UDV branch in New Mexico in 1993.

In 1993, then, the UDV and Santo Daime both existed in the United States, both imported their respective sacraments, and both distributed ayahuasca to the members of their communities. The groups were aware of each other's existence, but operated independently and followed their own production and importation protocols. Their fates became intertwined, however, in 1999, when customs agents seized ayahuasca shipments sent from Brazil to the respective communities.

Ayahuasca Religion in the United States after RFRA

As Lattin writes, Americans' interest in ayahuasca is growing exponentially in the twenty-first century.[30] That was not the case, however, in 1999, when comparably few Americans were familiar with ayahuasca, including the US Customs agents who seized a shipment destined for the UDV in New Mexico and another destined for Santo Daime in Oregon. Customs agents tested the liquids and found that they contained DMT, an illegal substance classified as a Schedule I drug under the CSA. Government agents subsequently executed search warrants on Bronfman and Goldman's properties. They seized thirty gallons of ayahuasca at Bronfman's residence and arrested Goldman.

The raids launched several prolonged legal battles. They also ignited a disagreement within the Santo Daime community that put Goldman at odds with group leaders, who advised Goldman not to pursue any legal remedy. In the wake of their disagreements, Goldman and his community continued to meet in private to minimize and potentially avoid lengthy legal disputes with the US government. Bronfman, however, fought back. He hired attorneys to represent him and his community, resulting in the aforementioned case, *O Centro Espírita Beneficiente* v. *Ashcroft*. As noted in Section 2, the Supreme Court would eventually hear this case in the form of *Gonzales* v. *O Centro Espírita Beneficente União do Vegetal*, where the court unanimously concluded, first, that RFRA applied to federal laws, and second, that RFRA's broad endorsement of religious freedom required the government to allow the UDV to import and to distribute hoasca to its members. In other words, for the first time in US history, the Supreme Court both acknowledged the legitimacy or the religiosity of the sacramental use of a psychoactive substance and determined that American jurisprudence required the government to sanction it, as least in this specific instance. The *Gonzales* case caught the attention of people across the political spectrum. Lawyers, scholars, and activists took notice, particularly attorneys

---

[30] Personal conversation with author, August 10, 2022.

like Greg Lake and Ian Benouis, who argued that this case, in conjunction with the lower courts' rulings that laid the foundation for this case, broadly empowers entheogenic communities.

União do Vegetal Goes to Court

As discussed earlier in this Element, *Gonzales* v. *O Centro Espírita Beneficente União do Vegetal* was the final version of a case that began in New Mexico under the name *O Centro Espírita Beneficiente* v. *Ashcroft*. In his writings, Greg Lake explores the *Ashcroft* decision, which the Court of Appeals for the Tenth Circuit heard and decided, instead of the *Gonzales* decision made by the Supreme Court. In *The Law of Entheogenic Churches*, Lake justified his decision to focus on the *Ashcroft* decision when he claimed, first, the main issues were present in the earlier *Ashcroft* case, and second, that the Supreme Court affirmed the lower court's decision. With that in mind, Lake explores the *Ashcroft* case at length.

In *O Centro Espírita Beneficiente* v. *Ashcroft*, the Court of Appeals for the Tenth Circuit heard arguments between the UDV and the Government. (The court capitalized the "G" in "government" presumably to highlight that Attorney General John Ashcroft represented the government itself. For consistency's sake, this Element will follow that capitalization structure – "government" means "government in general"; "Government" means "defendant in this case.") Lake began his analysis of *O Centro Espírita Beneficiente* v. *Ashcroft* by summarizing the UDV's history, the structure of UDV's ceremonies, and the UDV's belief that "UDV church doctrine dictates members only can perceive and understand God by drinking hoasca" (Lake 2021, 26). This history and the church's beliefs are important, first, because they allegedly demonstrate the group's religiosity, and second, because they allegedly establish that the government would impose a substantial burden on the church if it prevented the UDV from importing and consuming hoasca. This burden, as RFRA indicates, requires the government first to demonstrate a compelling governmental interest and then to take the least restrictive means of furthering that interest. Government attorneys were obviously aware of this, and Lake summarized several of the Government's arguments related to RFRA.

First, the Government could have challenged the religiosity of the UDV. That is, the Government could have maintained that the UDV was not a real or authentic religion. If the Government made that argument and persuaded the court, then further analysis would be moot. Instead, however, the Government ceded the issue without additional qualification. That is, the Government acknowledged that the UDV was a religion, but did not provide an extensive analysis or explanation of its logic. The courts similarly accepted the group's religiosity.

When the Government acknowledged the UDV's religious sincerity, however, it arguably triggered RFRA and its assertion that the Government cannot substantially burden the exercise of religion without a compelling governmental interest. The Government acknowledged that the seizure of hoasca imposed a substantial burden, but it also contended that it had not one, but three compelling reasons to impose this burden. Lake summarized the Government's three reasons when he wrote that the Government was concerned with

> (1) protection of the health and safety of União do Vegetal members; (2) potential for diversion of hoasca from the church to recreational users; and (3) compliance with the 1971 United Nations Convention on Psychotropic Substances (Convention). (Lake 2021, 27)

Individually or combined, the Government argued, these are the compelling state interests that allow the Government to substantially burden the UDV.

The UDV's attorneys responded to and rejected each of these arguments. These arguments are important for Lake and his clients because they demonstrate the court's concerns – concerns that Lake's clients can anticipate and preemptively address when they create their own communities. The first issue that Lake addressed is that of safety and health. This issue was central, first in the District Court hearing and then again at the Court of Appeals. The issue resurfaced when the Supreme Court heard the case. In all versions of this case, the various parties disagreed on the health and safety risks posed by hoasca, but they seemed to agree that the issue was of paramount importance, so both sides solicited the testimony of experts.

The Government argued that the consumption of hoasca posed a health and safety threat to UDV members. The UDV countered when they attempted to systematically dispute this. The problem, as the court noted, was that both sides had little quantitative research to bolster their claims. The court noted as much when it wrote, "The dearth of conclusive research on DMT and hoasca fuels the controversy in this case" (*O Centro Espírita Benficiente*, 342 F.3d at 1179).

To support their position that the UDV's consumption of hoasca posed no significant health or safety risks, the UDV presented evidence from a 1993 study led by Dr. Charles Grob, Professor of Psychiatry at the University of California, Los Angeles. Grob had conducted research where he "compared 15 long-term União do Vegetal members, who drank hoasca for several years, with 15 control subjects who never ingested the tea" (*O Centro Espírita Beneficiente*, 1179). Grob and his team completed various psychiatric, neuropsychological, and physical tests and interviews. The researchers published their findings, where they "reported a positive overall assessment of the safety of hoasca" (*O Centro Espírita Beneficiente*, 1179. See Grob et al., 1996). In his court testimony, Grob acknowledged the limits of his study, but added that the research

> did identify that in a group of randomly collected male subjects who had consumed ayahuasca for many years, entirely within the context of a very tightly organized syncretic church, there had been no injurious effects caused by their use of ayahuasca. On the contrary, our research team was consistently impressed with the very high functional status of the ayahuasca subjects. (*O Centro Espírita Beneficiente*, 1179)

The Government's response was multipointed. First, the Government argued, the fact that DMT is a Schedule I drug reflects Congressional findings that it "has a high potential for abuse . . . no currently accepted medical use [and] a lack of accepted safety for use under medical supervision" (21 U.S.C. § 812[b][1]). The Government also criticized Grob's study claiming methodological errors (it only studied males), selection bias, and limited sample size. Dr. Alexander Walker, Professor of Epidemiology at the Harvard School of Public Health, highlighted the issue of selection bias when he said that Grob failed to adequately account for controls in his assessment of the UDV members and the control group.[31]

The Government also solicited the testimony of Dr. Sander Genser – Chief of the Medical Consequences Unit of the Center on AIDS and Other Medical Consequences of Drug Abuse at the National Institutes of Health – who cited a study where two subjects were intravenously administered DMT. One "experienced a high rise in blood pressure, and another had a recurrence of depression" (*O Centro Espírita Beneficiente*, 1180). Genser also raised concerns about other hallucinogenics, particularly LSD, which "may produce prolonged psychotic reactions or posthallucinogen perceptual disorder, commonly known as 'flashbacks,' defined as the reemergence of some aspect of the hallucinogenic experience in the absence of the drug" (*O Centro Espírita Beneficiente*, 1180).

The UDV countered these various claims when they solicited the testimony of "UDV expert" Dr. David Nichols of Purdue University, Professor of Medical Chemistry and Molecular Pharmacology (*O Centro Espírita Beneficiente*, 1180). Nichols highlighted several differences between the study Genser cited

---

[31] The court summarized Walker's argument when it wrote, "According to Dr. Alexander Walker . . . the selection of long-term members of União do Vegetal, individuals who were able to conform to its norms over extended periods, without a similar requirement for stable, long-term, voluntary church attendance applied to the control group, ensured the hoasca-consuming group necessarily had a favorable psychological profile" (*O Centro Espírita Beneficiente*, 1181).

and the UDV's sacramental consumption of hoasca. Nichols argued that compared to intravenously administered DMT, "[o]rally ingested hoasca produces a less intense, more manageable, and inherently psychologically safer altered state of consciousness" (*O Centro Espírita Beneficiente*, 1180). He also questioned the association of hoasca with other hallucinogenics, and he highlighted the importance of "set and setting" when he argued "the ritual setting of União do Vegetal members' consumption minimizes danger and optimizes safety" (*O Centro Espírita Beneficiente*, 1180).

Despite their differences, both sides acknowledged that hoasca may pose adverse reactions when consumed by people on certain medications, particularly some antidepressants, which increase risk of serotonin syndrome, a potentially lethal condition. Genser also noted that "irreversible" MAOIs were particularly dangerous. The UDV responded by acknowledging some of these concerns. Because the group is aware of potential adverse drug interactions, they conduct health screenings and interview every member to ensure that they are not taking any problematic medications. The UDV also said that Genser's concerns about irreversible MAOIs were basically moot, as hoasca does not contain irreversible MAOIs. The UDV also argued that "the risk of adverse drug interaction associated with hoasca falls within the normal spectrum of concerns" (*O Centro Espírita Beneficiente*, 1181). Finally, the Government argued that hoasca can result in increased risk of psychotic episodes, a claim the UDV dismissed as "coincidental, rather than causal, and that the reported very low occurrence of psychosis among church members in Brazil is equal or less than the rate in the general population" (*O Centro Espírita Beneficiente*, 1181).

After reviewing the evidence, the court concluded that the evidence was "in equipoise" (*O Centro Espírita Beneficiente*, 1181) and therefore failed to meet RFRA's demand that the Government must demonstrate a compelling governmental interest when it substantially burdens the exercise of religion. Based on this judgment, the court dismissed the health and safety issue when it wrote, "The Government 'failed to build an adequate record' demonstrating danger to União do Vegetal members' health from sacramental hoasca use" (*O Centro Espírita Beneficiente*, 1181–2).

Having addressed the first of the Government's three–pronged attempt to justify a compelling government interest to prevent the UDV from importing and consuming hoasca, the focus shifted to the issue of diversion. As Lake observed, "in addition to health and safety of UDV members, the Government also advanced the argument, in an effort to show a compelling governmental interest, that hoasca used by the UDV would be vulnerable to diversion" (Lake 2021, 31–2). Over the next several pages in *The Law of Entheogenic Churches in the United States*, Lake summarized the back-and-forth arguments between, on the one side, the Government and its supporters, and on the other side, the UDV and its supporters.

The Government first solicited the testimony of Terrance Woodworth, Deputy Director of the Drug Enforcement Administration's Office of Diversion Control, who cited four factors the agency used to assess the diversion risk of a controlled substances: "the existence of an illicit market, the presence of marketing or publicity, the form of the substance, and the cost and opportunity of diversion" (Lake 2021, 32). Woodworth then applied these factors to hoasca, where he acknowledged that ayahuasca is not consumed in large amounts, but he also stated that increased interest in hallucinogenics in the United States is driving a greater demand in the underground market, which presumably increases the risk of diversion. He also said that, were the UDV granted the exemption it seeks, the "uncooperative relationship between the DEA and União do Vegetal" (*O Centro Espírita Beneficiente*, 1182) would also cause an increase in illegal diversion.

To address the potential risk of abuse, the Government also solicited the testimony of Dr. Miroslaw Janowski, Professor of Medicine at the Johns Hopkins School of Medicine. Janowski said that people who consume hoasca often report "positive reinforcing, or 'euphoric,' effects" (*O Centro Espírita Beneficiente*, 1182) – effects that people also report in studies of intravenously injected DMT and in preliminary studies on hoasca. These accounts, he concluded, will motivate people to consume hoasca. Janowski ceded that some people who consume hoasca report negative effects of vomiting and nausea and that these stories might dissuade some potential users; however, he also said that the percentage of people who describe negative effects is unknown, and that, all things considered, the reporting of negative effects will not deter users. Finally, Janowski argued that LSD and DMT are pharmacologically similar, indicating that hoasca has a high abuse potential.

The UDV rejected the Government's arguments and solicited the testimony of Dr. Mark Kleiman, Professor of Policy Studies at the University of California, Los Angeles, who testified that if the UDV received its exemption, the reporting of negative effects of hoasca and the availability of pharmacologically equivalent substitutes indicate demand for the substance would remain low (*O Centro Espírita Beneficiente*, 1182). Kleiman then offered four factors that would not increase the risk of diversion. According to Lake, these factors were

> (1) UDV in the United States is a very small church and would only import
> about 3,000 doses per year; (2) the relatively thin market for hoasca would
> reduce likelihood of diversion; (3) the bulky form of hoasca would deter

diversion; and (4) the UDV has strong incentives to keep its hoasca supply from being diverted as the consumption of the tea outside of the ceremonial context is considered sacrilegious. (Lake 2021, 34)

After hearing these arguments, the court concluded that "the evidence on the potential for diversion [w]as 'virtually balanced'" (*O Centro Espírita Beneficiente*, 1183). Given this balance, the court determined that the Government failed to demonstrate a compelling interest and that it failed "to meet the Government's onerous burden of proof" under RFRA (*O Centro Espírita Beneficiente*, 1183). In other words, the court rejected the second prong of the Government's three-pronged attempt to demonstrate a compelling governmental interest in substantially burdening the UDV's religiosity.

Having addressed the first two prongs, the focus turned to the third prong – The United Nations Convention on Psychotropic Substances. In contrast to his lengthy summary of the topics addressed in the previous two issues, Lake's analysis of this issue, at one paragraph, is comparably short. This brevity is evidenced by the fact that the court had little trouble addressing and dismissing it. Simply put, the Government stressed the importance of the UN's Convention and cited it as evidence of the Government's compelling state interest. The Court, however, argued that "Treaties are part of the law of the land; they have no greater or lesser impact than other federal laws" (*O Centro Espírita Beneficiente*, 1184). RFRA, the Court concluded, is one such federal law. Given the importance of religious freedom, the court concluded, the Government cannot invoke the United Nation's Convention to summarily override or dismiss RFRA, which "requires that an asserted compelling interest be narrowly tailored to the specific plaintiff whose religious conduct is impaired" (*O Centro Espírita Beneficiente*, 1184). "Based on the record before us," the court wrote, "we cannot conclude the Government has demonstrated that 'application of the burden to the [UDV] (1) is in furtherance of a compelling government interest; and (2) is the least restrictive means of furthering that compelling government interest'" (*O Centro Espírita Beneficiente*, 1184).

Having clearly ruled in the UDV's favor, the Court addressed several issues it referred to as "Additional Arguments" (*O Centro Espírita Beneficiente*, 1184). Lake devoted a significant amount of attention to this section of the Court's opinion, as he concluded that they will be relevant to future cases involving entheogenic communities. He wrote, "First, the Court observed the sincerity of the UDV's religious practice and the substantial burden placed thereon by the Controlled Substances Act were uncontested" (Lake 2021, 35). This is important because the Court could have questioned and even rejected the religiosity of the UDV. As the Court noted in its holding, there is precedent for denying a claimant's self-reported religiosity, as evidenced by the case *United States v. Meyers*, where the Court concluded that the defendant's beliefs "espouse a philosophy and/or way of life rather than a religion'" (*O Centro Espírita Beneficiente*, 1185). Despite this precedent, the Government and the various courts accepted prima facie the UDV's religiosity.

The court also highlighted a distinction between the UDV's sacramental use of hoasca and previous court decisions involving marijuana. According to Lake, the court highlighted this distinction to emphasize that the UDV only sanctions the use of hoasca in a "'traditional, precisely circumscribed ritual' where the drug 'itself is an object of worship; and using the sacrament outside of the religious context is sacrilege'" (Lake, 2021, 35). This explicitly ceremonial and sacrificial use of hoasca differentiates the UDV's case from earlier cases that addressed the religious use of marijuana, where defendants encouraged the consumption of marijuana outside religious contexts.

Finally, during the hearings, Government lawyers also argued for the importance of the "uniform application of the CSA, the need to avoid burdensome and constant official supervision and management of União do Vegetal, and the possibility of opening the door to myriad claims for religious exceptions" (*O Centro Espírita Beneficiente*, 1185–6). The court dismissed these concerns, arguing, respectively, that RFRA required the state to consider an exception, that an exception from the CSA might actually turn the relationship between the DEA and the UDV from "adversarial" to "a cooperative relationship" (*O Centro Espírita Beneficiente*, 1186), and that "the bald assertion of a torrent of religious exemptions does not satisfy the Government's RFRA burden" (*O Centro Espírita Beneficiente*, 1187).

Lake elaborated on these issues when he noted, first, that the US Supreme Court upheld the court's verdict in *O Centro Espírita Beneficiente* v. *Ashcroft*. He also noted that the exemption from the CSA requires the UDV to work with the DEA, the latter of which issued the UDV a licensing number, which requires "the church to keep meticulously record[ed] the amounts of ayahuasca both imported and consumed, as well as requiring strict substance handling procedures" (Lake 2021, 36). He also reminded readers that the DEA can randomly inspect and test hoasca. In other words, the court's decision does not grant the UDV the right to operate independently of the DEA. Instead, the exemption initiates a requirement for engagement. "Therefore," Lake wrote, "once an RFRA claimant wins in federal court, the relief is to obtain a DEA license number and begin DEA monitoring" (Lake 2021, 36). This will become important because it has shaped the legal counsel he subsequently provided to his clients.

Santo Daime Goes to Court

The UDV was one of two communities that had their ayahuasca seized in 1999. The other community, the Oregon Santo Daime community, went underground and held their ceremonies in private while the UDV's cases played out in the courts. When the Supreme Court sided in the UDV's favor in 2006, however, the Santo Daime community in Oregon similarly sued the government for the right to import, distribute to members, and consume Daime (readers will recall that members of Santo Daime refer to ayahuasca as "Daime"). This case also influences the advice that Lake provides to his entheogenic clients.

This case, *Church of the Holy Light of the Queen v. Mukasey* (615 F.Supp.2d 1210, 2009), involved two Santo Daime communities in Oregon – the Church of the Holy Light of the Queen led by Jonathan Goldman, and the Céu da Divina Rosa in Portland, led by plaintiff Alexandra Bliss Yeager. Judge Owen Murphy Panner heard this case in the US District Court in Oregon, which issued its decision in 2009. Overall, this case resembled the UDV case in several important ways. Specifically, the Government admitted that preventing Santo Daime practitioners from consuming Daime would substantially burden their religion; the Government argued that it had compelling governmental interests to burden Santo Daime's religion; and each side offered expert testimonies to support their arguments. The difference between the cases lies in a combination of comparably minor details together with the looming presence of the unanimous Supreme Court decision in the UDV case.

In his decision, Judge Panner began by acknowledging that Jonathan Goldman was the group's spiritual leader and that he was religiously sincere (*Church of the Holy Light of the Queen*, 1212). Judge Panner summarized the evidence for Goldman's sincerity when he wrote

> Goldman has been studying the Santo Daime religion for 21 years, traveling frequently to Brazil to receive instruction from church leaders. He has learned Portuguese to understand the Santo Daime hymns that constitute church doctrine. Goldman has been an initiate of the Santo Daime church for almost 19 years. He founded CHLQ in 1993 with authorization from the Santo Daime mother church in Brazil. (*Church of the Holy Light of the Queen*, 1212)

Based on these facts, Judge Panner recognized Goldman's testimony to be sincerely religious, and he reached a similar conclusion about Yeager and the other plaintiffs. Panner then recapitulated Santo Daime's history, its spread to the United States, and the Government's actions that precipitated the case.

Panner then summarized how the Government presented two reasons to substantially burden the UDV's religiosity – members' health and safety and the risk of diversion (unlike the UDV case, the Government did not cite the UN Convention). The details of these arguments resemble the arguments in the UDV case, with a few subtle distinctions. The Government, for example, continued to imply guilt by association when it drew parallels between Daime and drugs like LSD and injected DMT, arguments the Oregon judge dismissed as "marginally relevant" (*Church of the Holy Light of the Queen*, 1215). The Government also cited Daime drinkers who experience anxiety, discomfort, nausea, vomiting, diarrhea, high blood pressure, and increases in heart rate (*Church of the Holy Light of the Queen*, 1215). In response, Santo Daime and supporting experts alleged that no one had died from consuming Daime, that they had extensive screening processes, that several members are physicians and nurses, and that they have assigned "Guardians" who help people in distress during ceremonies. They also cited more recent studies and the testimony of Santo Daime members, concluding persuasively that Santo Daime took appropriate health and safety measures and protocols.

In other words, the arguments over health and safety in this case resembled the arguments in the UDV case. Despite these similarities, some differences are worth noting. Several Santo Daime members admitted to smoking marijuana, and during the Government's raid in 1999, the Government found a small amount of marijuana in Goldman's bedroom. Additionally, Santo Daime admitted giving Daime to children; and Government lawyers raised the possibility that a fetus might be harmed if a pregnant woman consumed Daime.

Panner rejected all these arguments as compelling reasons to substantially burden Santo Daime's religiosity. Regarding the marijuana in Goldman's bedroom, plaintiffs said that the marijuana belonged to Goldman's wife, who used it medicinally. "Regardless of why marijuana was in Goldman's bedroom nearly ten years ago," Panner wrote, "a spiritual leader's possible personal failings should not discredit the entire church" (*Church of the Holy Light of the Queen*, 1214). Regarding the members who consumed marijuana, Judge Panner noted that the founder of Santo Daime briefly allowed its ritual use, although the church had since affirmed its commitment to being a one-sacrament church (*Church of the Holy Light of the Queen*, 1214). Panner also remarked that many of the members who consumed marijuana stated a desire to stop. Finally, the judge said that the Government failed to present any compelling evidence that a fetus could be harmed by the consumption of Daime.

The Government next addressed the issue of diversion. Judge Panner devoted only 155 words to addressing this issue, suggesting that he felt the Government's arguments were easily dismissed. As he noted, only three or four people in the church have access to the Daime, the Government was not able to provide any evidence that Santo Daime ever allowed anyone to consume

Daime without the church's authorization, and the church considered the use of Daime outside ceremony a violation of church doctrines (*Church of the Holy Light of the Queen*, 1217). The judge also concluded that the Government failed to provide evidence that a viable market existed for Daime.

Based on these arguments, Judge Panner replicated the Supreme Court's logic in the UDV case when he applied RFRA, analyzed the details of this case, and concluded that the Government failed to meet its burden under RFRA to provide a compelling governmental interest to substantially burden Santo Daime's religiosity. "Plaintiffs are entitled to relief under RFRA," Panner concluded (*Church of the Holy Light of the Queen*, 1221). "Judgment will be entered for plaintiffs in accordance with this opinion."

"The Takeaway"

In *The Law of Entheogenic Churches in the United States*, Lake summarized the importance and relevance of these two cases in a section he titled The Takeaway. This section is particularly important because Lake himself is a consumer of entheogens, an entheogenic activist, and the legal counsel to dozens of entheogenic consumers. This is a person who, in his own words, works "non-stop ... to push the movement ahead" (Lake 2021, vi). The Takeaway then, is a short but succinct summary of the legal advice that Lake provides to entheogenic consumers and organizers across the country. This advice is based on Lake's interpretation of the existing cases and laws that, in his mind, offer the strongest support for the legality of entheogenic drug use.

Lake organized The Takeaway into three large categories, each with multiple subpoints. All three categories reference one of RFRA's first two prongs. Based on his interpretation of the relevant court cases, Lake began by listing seven factors that helped the courts recognize entheogenic religiosity. They include, first, the simple reminder that the courts have recognized the religiosity of entheogenic sacraments consumed to "commune with higher spiritual forces or entities" (Lake 2021, 46). Second, that courts will deny a claimant's religiosity if the courts believe "RFRA is being used as a shield from prosecution" (Lake, 2021, 47). Third, that courts have denied the religiosity or the religious sincerity of people consuming entheogens "outside of the ceremonial context, as part of a purported religion" (Lake 2021, 47). Fourth, that the DEA has a history of threatening legal action, of raiding leaders' homes, and of questioning the religiosity of leaders who stop holding ceremonies or who hold ceremonies in secret. "Best practice," Lake wrote, "is to always to continue safely exercising one's sincerely held religious beliefs" (Lake 2021, 47). Fifth, Lake reminded readers that the courts do not agree on tests or models to use to determine religiosity, but rather the *Meyers* decision and the "functional approach" seem to be the most common tests. Lake seems to believe the *Meyers* criteria are the most effective. "Using the *Meyers* factors," he wrote, "is a great way to structure a belief system as it provides a framework most closely linked to traditional religions and therefore is more easily identifiable as 'religious' to most judges" (Lake 2021, 47). Sixth, Lake succinctly reminds his readers, "Do not mock established religions . . . it never ends well" (Lake 2021, 47). Finally, Lake emphasizes that the presence of "'non-sacramental' substances found on church property can and will be used by the government to try and controvert the sincerity of the religious exercise" (Lake 2021, 47).

The final two sections of The Takeaway addressed RFRA's claim that the government must demonstrate a compelling governmental interest to burden religion. To that end, Lake encouraged readers to consider ten points. First, Lake contended that recent research has demonstrated that when consumed in religious sets and settings, ayahuasca and other entheogenic sacraments are safe. Also, Lake concluded that the courts' recognition and subsequent approval of entheogenic sacraments seems contingent on church leaders who create and implement extensive screening processes to identify and prohibit from ceremonies people who have medical risks, mental health risks, and people who are not interested in the sacramental consumption of these substances. Courts are more likely to support entheogenic communities, Lake argued, when church doctrine forbids the nonreligious use of entheogenic sacraments outside church rituals. Additionally, Lake wrote that the leader, shaman, and facilitators should monitor ceremonies, and if possible, a medically trained person should be present. Lake also listed several criteria that influence the DEA's assessment of risk of diversion, including the "existence of an illicit market; presence of marketing and publicity; form of the substance; and cost and opportunity of diversion" (Lake 2021, 48). Lake also cautioned people to consider the potential for the abuse of the sacrament, the existence of pharmacologically similar substitutes for specific sacraments, and the number of doses served and ingested.

Based on these factors, Lake wrote a separate chapter titled, "General Guide to Forming a Non-Profit Church" (Lake 2021, 65–76). This guide is particularly important because it reflects Lake's desire to create churches that model the ayahuasca churches that the courts have already approved. In other words, Lake advises his clients to replicate the styles of religiosity and the model of religious communities that have successfully sought relief under RFRA. This replication, he wrote, includes "formalities that can offer greater protection" for entheogenic communities (Lake 2021, 65). More than any other place in his books, this chapter stresses the importance of conformity and imitation as it discourages innovation.

Lake began this chapter by acknowledging that American courts tend to favor a church or organizational model of religiosity. Scholars have long noted different models of religiosity; however, due largely to the Christian bias in American jurisprudence (see Sullivan et al. 2015), Lake concluded that American courts are more likely to recognize something as religious when it operates under the auspices of an official organization.[32] To this end, Lake advised readers to form churches by completing the paperwork at the state level. This paperwork requires the church to have a board of directors and a registered agent. This agent, he wrote, "can be someone involved in the management of the non-profit but does not necessarily have to be involved" (Lake 2021, 67). This agent will complete the requisite paperwork to create either a 501(c)(3) or 508(c)(1)(a) organization. If someone creates the former, the IRS will consider additional information before it grants that the organization is authentically religious. For this reason, Lake prefers that his clients incorporate as 508(c)(1) (a) organizations, which he contends, "Is specifically for non-profit 'faith-based' organizations" (Lake 2021, 69). The benefit of forming the organization with this code is that the IRS more readily accepts the group's religiosity, where a 501(c)(3) has to answer a questionnaire of sorts to demonstrate its religiosity. He concludes, "508(c)(1)(a) is pretty much a default provision whereby a non-profit church can operate as tax-exempt but escape the rigors of qualifying as 'church' under 501(c)(3)" (Lake 2021, 70).

Lake also advises churches to create several documents commonly associated with institutional religion and therefore favored by the courts. "As a practical matter," he wrote, "I usually advise my clients to use the *Meyers* factors when drafting their internal church documents, as it provides a good framework for elucidating the statement of beliefs" (Lake 2021, 15–16). These include, first, bylaws, which address a comprehensive list of administrative positions, administrative responsibilities, and administrative policies. Lake also advises that churches create a statement of faith. Each statement should reference ultimate ideas, metaphysical beliefs, moral or ethical systems, comprehensiveness of beliefs, and many of the ten "accoutrements of religion." Each statement, when possible, should also reference factors addressed in relevant

---

[32] Communities besides Christianity operate with organizational models of religiosity. Scholars have documented, however, that judges and courts in the United States are predominantly motivated by notions of religiosity common in Christianity (again, see Sullivan et al. 2015). This is hardly surprising given, first, that Christians have been a majority in the nation since its founding, and second, since the category of "religion" itself is modeled after Christianity (Schilbrack 2022).

court cases such as diversion, health and safety, and sacrament handling and storage policies. His advice is deliberately designed to benefit entheogenic groups, although this advice in theory would benefit any group that considers itself a new or emerging religion and that wants the government to acknowledge it as such.

In short, Lake recognizes that his clients are engaging in risky behaviors and he advises his clients to minimize risk by replicating the models of religiosity the courts have previously sanctioned. This replication, he contends, provides the greatest protections, but it does require the practitioners to fashion churches and communities they otherwise would not create, and to craft them in styles based on precedent. Lee Armstrong, for example, is the founder of an ayahuasca church who spoke rather candidly about this process. "How would I have done things differently if I could," he asked as he repeated my question.

> I'd probably do a lot different. When I trained to be a shaman in Peru, there weren't any churches involved. It was my teacher, his family, and other people who came and went for ceremony. No paperwork, no government approval, no bylaws, no statements of faith; just a man and his family providing ceremony to a rotating group of people. If I could, I'd probably do something like that. I'd just advertise to get the word out and hold ceremony. I wouldn't have to keep records, have a freakin' board of directors, and deal with the government bullshit. I mean, I'll still do some of what [Lake] advised – things like keeping the sacrament safe. And that's another thing – I wouldn't use the word sacrament. It's not that I don't believe it's a sacrament, it's just that that isn't my first choice of words. We typically call it "the medicine," and while the medical side of aya assumes a sacred or supernatural element, "sacrament" just isn't my first word. So yeah, I'd protect the sacrament, but I doubt I'd call it that. I mean, I'll do all this, because I have to, but I just wish we could just be ourselves and not feel like we're roleplaying or whatever. I also wish I had the freedom to offer more than one sacrament. It's like I only get religious freedom when I'm not authentic, you know? It's like wearing a straitjacket sometimes.[33]

Armstrong expressed many of the concerns that founders of other communities shared. Particularly, they feel burdened by the organizational model, by the paperwork, and by the specific ways they feel pressure to demonstrate religious sincerity in a way the courts would recognize. Another founder of an entheogenic community addressed an additional issue that bothers her.

Theresa Restivo is the founder of a psilocybin church. "One of the main things we worry about," she said, "is making sure we check the boxes, so to speak, with community events and engagements. We like having community

---

[33] Personal conversation with author, October 13, 2022.

get togethers and all, but we're always feeling pressured to have more, you know. How many are enough? And when we do meet, we feel pressured to look more religiony than we'd like to" (Restivo 2023). Restivo is particularly concerned with the details of their community meetings. "Like, we have to start with a prayer because Christians pray, we have to find something to read because Christians have their Bibles, we have to, you know, fit the mold, no? Obviously, we do the things we need to, but it doesn't always feel natural. More contrived at times."

My conversations with Armstrong and Restivo reveal common themes that emerged in my research with white founders of entheogenic communities. First, they acknowledge the pressure they feel to look and act certain ways. They harbor various degrees of resentment about this pressure, but they also agree to heed their attorneys' advice. Restivo described a common response to all of this when she said:

> Whenever I feel like it's too much – too burdensome – I think about the contrary, or, what are my other options? I need to serve the sacrament to my community and I need to stay out of jail. If this is how I accomplish those goals, I'm happy – more or less – to play the game. I mean, maybe I should say that I'm willing to play the game, but it is tiring.[34]

Ethnographic research with many of the founders of these communities suggests that most of these founders would agree.

4 Conclusion

Studies conducted in the twenty-first century by organizations like the Pew Research Center document the historically unprecedented rise in "Nones," or people who claim no religious affiliation (Smith 2021). Many of these individuals consider themselves spiritual but not religious (SBNR), in that they continue to embrace and believe in ideas commonly associated with religion, and they practice rituals that themselves are often associated with religion (Burge 2021). For various reasons, however, they distance themselves from the organized and institutional religions that have been omnipresent since European colonizers established the first churches in North America. The Nones and the SBNR, then, are not abandoning their beliefs in the supernatural; they are instead rejecting religious institutions and the taxonomic category of religion itself.

Despite this larger trend, many Americans are once again finding religion in new formal and institutionalized churches based on the sacramental consumption of otherwise illegal psychoactive substances. The members of these

---

[34] Personal conversation with author, March 5, 2023.

communities continue to invoke their spirituality, but they also regularly and deliberately use the word "religion" to describe their communities – communities registered with the state and federal government as either 501(c)(3) or 508(c)(1)(a) nonprofit churches. These churches challenge dominant understandings of religion and religiosity when they associate their practices with the sacramental consumption of entheogens, but in many other ways, they are copying models of religiosity long recognized as religion both by the courts and by North Americans more broadly. These models include formal religious institutions, statements of faith, official church membership rolls, membership dues or tithes, bylaws, regularly scheduled services and ceremonies, and extra-curricular activities outside these services and ceremonies. In other words, these models resemble Old-Time Religion with one notable exception – the sacramental consumption of entheogenic substances.

These similarities are not coincidental; rather, they are by design and are the result of deliberate decisions the founders of these communities committed to when they created these churches. These churches are founded by entheogenic entrepreneurs who consult attorneys like Greg Lake and Ian Benouis, who interpret existing laws and court cases and who then advise their clients to reproduce the models of entheogenic churches the courts have previously sanctioned. This replication, they contend, does not guarantee legal immunity, but it does provide the strongest legal support in the event of government intervention.

As this Element suggests, these new entheogenic churches are not organic. Like all social formations, various sociocultural, political, economic, and legal factors influence their organizational structure and administrative operations. By design, they resemble the Christian-influenced ayahuasca communities that emerged in Brazil and that subsequently spread to the United States and convinced the courts of their religious sincerity. To understand these influences, consider the historical and archaeological records that indicate that prior to European colonialism, there were no formal entheogenic churches or organizations. Instead, people consumed psychoactive substances in a variety of settings and patterns. These paradigms involved structured rituals provided by trained providers, but these rituals and providers did not operate in the state-sanctioned institutional model that emerged after the formation of the nation-state and its bureaucratic and administrative structures. Additionally, while researching in Peru and Ecuador in the summers of 2022 and 2023, I witnessed and participated in rituals administered by people who seemingly lack formalized training, but who harvested psychoactive plants and performed private rituals. Given the structure of these postcolonial Indigenous societies today and the ubiquitous access to psychoactive plants, it is reasonable to infer that similar ceremonies existed prior to colonialism.

In other words, historical records and ethnographic research suggest that while psychoactive substances were (and continue to be) consumed in ceremonial settings of various sizes, the consumption of these substances was not associated with institutional religions or with churches that create bylaws, statements of faith, membership rolls, or many of the other so-called accoutrements of religion. In the twentieth century, however, mestizo Brazilian Christians entered the Brazilian rainforest where they encountered ayahuasca. They incorporated the consumption of ayahuasca into the churches they created and modeled after Christian churches. Around the year 1990, these churches spread to the United States where two of them became embroiled in legal battles over the legality of their religion. In the twenty-first century, the courts ultimately validated and upheld the groups' ability to import, to distribute, and consume their sacraments, but that validation and support was contingent on the group's religiosity. The courts had little problem identifying this religiosity, as it presented itself in distinctly recognizable forms. That is, Christian-inspired ayahuasca communities resembled the Christian models of religious practice that inform judges' opinions of religiosity writ large. Entheogenic churches, and their advocates, are now copying these models to create a new generation of Christian-imitative entheogenic communities.

The people in these communities are willing to repackage these models of religiosity for the sake of navigating the complex and high-stakes legal implications of practicing their beliefs and traditions, but one need only speculate cursorily to imagine alternate models of entheogenic community and consumption. These alternate models exist across the nation, and for the people who reject the court-sanctioned models, their refusal to at least attempt to resemble court-approved religiosity puts them at greater risk of arrest and incarceration. Other entheogenic practitioners, however, replicate the church model of religiosity. The heavy hand of the law looms over all these people, and for the sake of avoiding legal battles and imprisonment, some people are content to shake that hand, so to speak, even if it brings with it the burdensome weight of the hand itself.

Bibliography

Adams, D. W. (1995). *Education for Extinction: American Indians and the Boarding School Experience, 1875–1928*. Lawrence, KS: University of Kansas Press.

Alahmari, A. F. (2022). Neuroimaging Documentation of Psychedelic Drugs' Effect on the Brain: DMT, LSD, Psilocybin, and Ibogaine as Examples: A Mini Review. *Journal of Brain and Neurological Disorders*, 4(1), 1–9.

Aldred, L. (2000). Plastic Shamans and Astroturf Sun Dances: New Age Commercialization of Native American Spirituality. *American Indian Quarterly*, 24(3), 329–52.

Alexander, M. (2010). *The New Jim Crow: Mass Incarceration in the Age of Colorblindness*. New York, NY: New Press.

Allegro, J. M. (2009). *The Sacred Mushroom and Cross*. Garden City, NY: Gnostic Media.

Arie, E., B. Rosen, & D. Namdar (2020). Cannabis and Frankincense at the Judahite Shrine of Arad. *Journal of the Institute of Archaeology of Tel Aviv University*, 47(1), 5–28.

Arnal, W. E., & McCutcheon, R. T. (2013). *The Sacred Is the Profane: The Political Nature of "Religion."* New York, NY: Oxford University Press.

Arregi, J. I. (2021). Plastic Shamans, Intellectual Colonialism and Intellectual Appropriation in New Age Movements. *The International Journal of Ecopsychology*, 2(1), article 10.

Badliner, A. H. (2002). *Zig Zag Zen: Buddhism and Psychedelics*. San Francisco, CA: Chronicle Books.

Barnard, G. W. (2022). *Liquid Light: Ayahuasca Spirituality and the Santo Daime Tradition*. New York, NY: Columbia University Press.

Baum, D. (1996). *Smoke and Mirrors: The War on Drugs and the Politics of Failure*. Boston, MA: Back Bay Books.

Beltrán Peralta, N., Aulet, N., & Vidal-Casellas, D. (2022). Wine and Monasteries: Benedictine Monasteries in Europe. *Journal of Foodservice Business Research*, 25(6), 652–83.

Beyer, S. V. (2009) *Singing to the Plants: A Guide to Mestizo Shamanism in the Upper Amazon*. Albuquerque, NM: University of New Mexico Press.

Breen, B. (2019). *The Age of Intoxication: Origins of the Global Drug Trade*. Philadelphia, PA: University of Pennsylvania Press.

Burge, R. P. (2021). *The Nones: Where They Came From, Who They Are, and Where They Are Going*. Minneapolis, MN: Fortress Press.

Centro Espírita Beneficente União do Vegetal (2023). Available at: https:// udvusa.org/. Accessed August 18, 2023.

Chidester, D. (2014). *Empire of Religion Imperialism and Comparative Religion*. Chicago, IL: University of Chicago Press.

Crenshaw, K. (1989). Demarginalizing the Intersection of Race and Sex: A Black Feminist Critique of Antidiscrimination Doctrine, Feminist Theory and Antiracist Politics. *University of Chicago Legal Forum*, 1, article 8, 139–67.

Crowley, M. (2019). *Secret Drugs of Buddhism: Psychedelic Sacraments and the Origins of the Vajrayana*. Santa Fe, NM: Synergetic Press.

Curtis, F. (2016). *The Production of American Religious Freedom*. New York, NY: New York University Press.

Dallas, K. (2023). The Law That Changed Religious Freedom Forever. *Deseret News*, Nov. 15. www.deseret.com/2023/11/15/23942010/religious-freedom-restoration-act.

Dawson, A. (2013). *Santo Daime: A New World Religion*. New York, NY: Bloomsbury.

Dawson, A. (2018). *The Peyote Effect: From the Inquisition to the War on Drugs*. Berkeley, CA: University of California Press.

De la Torre, J. (2022). Oakland's psychedelic mushroom church makes a cautious return. *The Oaklandside*, June 10. Accessed online, August 28, 2023. https://oaklandside.org/2022/06/10/zide–door–psycedelic–magic–mushroom–church–oakland/.

Dirks, N. B. (2001). *Castes of Mind: Colonialism and the Making of Modern India*. Princeton, NJ: Princeton University Press.

Dobkin de Rios, M., & Grob, C. S. (2005). Interview with Jeffrey Bronfman, Representative Mestre for the União do Vegetal Church in the United States. *Journal of Psychoactive Drugs*, 37(2), 189–91.

Duvall, C. S. (2019). *The African Roots of Marijuana*. Durham, NC: Duke University Press.

Eisgruber, C. L., & Sager, L. G. (1994). Why the Religious Freedom Restoration Act is Unconstitutional. *New York University Law Review*, 69(3), 437–76.

Fernandes Antunes, H. (2023). Church of the *Holy Light of the Queen* v. *Mukasey*: The Regulation of a Santo Daime Church in the State of Oregon. In *Religious Freedom and the Global Regulation of Ayahuasca*, B. C. Labate and C. Clavar (eds.). New York, NY: Routledge, 38–50.

Fitzgerald, T. (2007). *Discourse on Civility and Barbarity*. New York, NY: Oxford University Press.

Fotiou, E. (2010). "From Medicine Men to Day Trippers: Shamanic Tourism in Iquitos, Peru." Ph.D. diss., University of Wisconsin–Madison.

Garland, D., ed. (2001). *Mass Imprisonment: Social Causes and Consequences*. London: SAGE.

Greenfield, R. (2006). *Timothy Leary: A Biography*. New York, NY: Harcourt.

Griffiths, R. R., Richards, W. A., McCann, U., & Jesse, R. (2006). Psilocybin Can Occasion Mystical-Type Experiences Having Substantial and Sustained Personal Meaning and Spiritual Significance. *Psychopharmacology*, 187(3), 268–83.

Grob, C. S., McKenna D. J., Callaway, J. C. Brito, G. S., Neves, E. S., Oberlaender, G., Saide, O. L., Labigalini, E., Tacla, C., Miranda, C. T., Strassman, R. J., & Boone, K. B. (1996). Human Psychopharmacology of Hoasca, a Plant Hallucinogen Used in Ritual Context in Brazil. *Journal of Nervous and Mental Disease*, 184(2), 86–94.

Gunther, M. (2020). No, Richard Nixon did not call Timothy Leary "the most dangerous man in America": At least there's no evidence that he did. *The Psychedelic Renaissance*, December 6. Accessed online, August 18, 2023. https://medium.com/the–psychedelic–renaissance/no–richard–nixon–did–not–call–timothy–leary–the–most–dangerous–man–in–america–72d04d6bb611.

Hamill, J., Hallak, J., Dursun, S. M., & Bakera G. (2019). Ayahuasca: Psychological and Physiologic Effects, Pharmacology and Potential Uses in Addiction and Mental Illness. *Current Neuropharmacology*, 17(2), 108–28.

Hamilton, M. (1998). The Religious Freedom Restoration Act is Unconstitutional. Period. *University of Pennsylvania Journal of Constitutional Law*, 1(1), 1–19.

Hamilton, M. (2005). *God vs. the Gavel: The Perils of Extreme Religious Liberty*. New York, NY: Cambridge University Press.

Harrison, P. (1990). *Religion and the Religions in the English Enlightenment*. Cambridge, UK: Cambridge University Press.

Hartogsohn, I. (2017). Constructing Drug Effects: A History of Set and Setting. *Drug Science, Policy and Law*, 3 (January–December). Accessed online, August 18, 2023. https://journals.sagepub.com/doi/epub/10.1177/2050324516683325.

Higgs, J. (2006). *I Have America Surrounded: A Biography of Timothy Leary*. Fort Lee, NJ: Barricade Books.

Hobson, G. (2002). The Rise of the White Shaman: Twenty-Five Years Later. *Studies in American Indian Literatures*, 14(2/3), 1–11.

Hodges, D. (2022). Spirituality & Beyond #2. *Church of Ambrosio YouTube Channel*. Accessed online, August 18, 2023. www.youtube.com/watch?v=N–I8XK8h–zI&t=53s.

Hofmann, A. (2009). *LSD, My Problem Child: Reflections on Sacred Drugs, Mysticism, and Science.* New York: McGraw-Hill Book Company.

Horii, M. (2020). Problems of "Religion" in Japan: Part 1 and 2. *Religion Compass* 14(11), 1–10.

Hughes, A. W. (2012). *Abrahamic Religions: On the Uses and Abuses of History.* New York, NY: Oxford University Press.

Hutchison, B. L. (2022). Revisiting *Employment Division* v. *Smith. University of Cincinnati Law Review,* 91(2), 396–436.

Jakobsen, J. R., & Pelligrini A. (2003). *Love the Sin: Sexual Regulation and the Limits of Religious Tolerance.* Boston, MA: Beacon Press.

Jama-Everett, A. (2021). Understanding Entheogens Podcast #1, June 12. Accessed Dec. 28, 2023. https://www.critical.consulting/post/understanding-entheogens-podcast-4-ayize-jama-everett.

James, W. (1902). *The Varieties of Religious Experience: A Study in Human Nature. Being the Gifford Lectures on Natural Religion Delivered at Edinburgh in 1901–1902.* New York, NY: Longman, Green, and Co.

Jay, M. (2019). *Mescaline: A Global History of the First Psychedelic.* New Haven, CT: Yale University Press.

Jay, M. (2023). *Psychonauts: Drugs and the Making of the Modern Mind.* New Haven, CT: Yale University Press.

Jesse Lee, Y. (2023). What to know about the booming psychedelics industry, where companies are racing to turn magic mushrooms and MDMA into approved medicines. *Business Insider,* March 9. Accessed online, February 23, 2024. https://www.businessinsider.com/psychedelics-industry-growth-pitch-deck-ipo-ceo-interviews.

Jiménez-Garrido, D. F., Gómez-Sousa, M., Ona, G., Dos Santos, R. G., Hallak, J. E. C., Alcázar-Córcoles, M. A., & Bouso, J. C. (2020). Effects of Ayahuasca on Mental Health and Quality of Life in Naïve Users: A Longitudinal and Cross-sectional Study Combination. *Scientific Reports,* 10, 1–12.

Johnstad, P. G. (2023). Racial and Religious Motives for Drug Criminalization. *Drug Science, Policy, and Law,* 9, 1–17.

Joneborg, I., Y. Lee, J. D. Di Vincenzo, F. Ceban, S. Meshkat, L. M. W. Lui, F. Fancy, J. D. Rosenblat, and R. S. McIntyre (2022). Active Mechanisms of Ketamine-Assisted Psychotherapy: A Systematic Review. *Journal of Affective Disorders* 315(15), 105–12.

Jordan, D. J. (2002). "An Offering of Wine: An Introductory Exploration of the Role of Wine in the Hebrew Bible and Ancient Judaism through the Examination of the Semantics of Some Keywords." Ph.D. diss., University of Sydney.

Khalifa, A. (1975). Traditional Patterns of Hashish Use in Egypt. In V. Rubin (ed.), *Cannabis and Culture*. Paris: Mouton, pp. 195–205.

Krupitsky, E. M., & A. Y. Grinenko (1997). Ketamine Psychedelic Therapy (KPT): A Review of the Results of Ten Years of Research. *Journal of Psychoactive Drugs* 29(2), 165–83.

Kuddus, M., I., Ginawi A. M., & Al–Hazimi, A. (2013). *Cannabis Sativa*: An Ancient Wild Edible Plant of India. *Emirates Journal of Food & Agriculture*, 25(10), 736–45.

Labate, B. C., & Cavnar, C. (2016). *Peyote: History, Tradition, Politics, and Conservation*. Santa Barbara, CA: ABC–CLIO.

Labate, B. C., & Cavnar, C. (2021). *Ayahuasca Healing and Science*. New York, NY: Springer.

Labate, B. C., Jungaberle, H., eds. (2011). *The Internationalization of Ayahuasca*. New York, NY: LIT Verlag.

Labate, B. C., MacRae, E., & Goulart, S. L. (2010). Brazilian Ayahuasca Religions in Perspective. In B. C. Labate & E. MacRae (eds.), *Ayahuasca, Ritual and Religion in Brazil*. London: Equinox, 1–20.

Lake, G. G. (2021). *The Law of Entheogenic Churches in the United States. Volume 1*. Self-published.

Lake, G. G. (2022). *The Law of Entheogenic Churches in the United States. Volume 2*. Self-published.

Lake, G. G. (2023). Greg Lake: The Church of Psilomethoxin Interview. Plus Three Podcast, May 9.

Lattin, D. (2010). *The Harvard Psychedelic Club: How Timothy Leary, Ram Dass, Huston Smith, and Andrew Weil Killed the Fifties and Ushered in a New Age for America*. New York, NY: HarperOne.

Lattin, D. (2012). *Distilled Spirits Getting High, Then Sober, with a Famous Writer, a Forgotten Philosopher, and a Hopeless Drunk*. Berkeley: University of California Press.

Lattin, D. (2017). *Changing Our Minds: Psychedelic Sacraments and the New Psychotherapy*. Santa Fe, NM: Synergetic Press.

Lattin, D. (2023). *God on Psychedelics: Tripping Across the Rubble of Old-Time Religion*. Hannacroix, NY: Apocryphile Press.

Laycock, D. (1998). Conceptual Gulfs in *City of Boerne v. Flores*. *William & Mary Law Review*, 39(3), 743–92.

Laycock, D. (2018). *Religious Liberty: Volume Four*. Grand Rapids, MI: Eerdman's Publishing Co.

Leary, T. (1967). *Start Your Own Religion*. Millbrook, NY: League for Spiritual Discovery.

Leary, T. (1968). *High Priest*. New York, NY: The World Publishing Company.

Leary, T., Metzner, R., & Alpert, R. (1964). *The Psychedelic Experience: A Manual Based on the Tibetan Book of the Dead*. New York, NY: University Books.

Lee, M. A., & Shlain, B. (2007). *Acid Dreams: The Complete Social History of LSD: The CIA, the Sixties, and Beyond*. New York, NY: Grove Press.

Letcher, A. (2007). *Shroom: A Cultural History of the Magic Mushroom*. New York, NY: HarperCollins.

Lewis, A. (2017). *The Rights Turn in Conservative Christian Politics: How Abortion Transformed the Culture Wars*. Cambridge, UK: Cambridge University Press.

Lindquist, G. E. E. (1923). *The Red Man in the United States: An Intimate Study of the Social, Economic, and Religious Life of the American Indian*. New York, NY: George H. Doran Company.

Lucia, A. J. (2020). *White Utopias: The Religious Exoticism of Transformational Festivals*. Berkeley: University of California Press.

Lupu, I. C. (1993). *Employment Division v. Smith* and the Decline of Supreme Court – Centrism. *BYU Law Review*, 1, 259–74.

Lupu, I. C., & R. Tuttle (2011). The Forms and Limits of Religious Accommodation: The Case of RLUIPA. *Cardozo Law Review*, 32, 1907–36.

Lutkajtis, A. (2021). Entity Encounters and the Therapeutic Effect of the Psychedelic Mystical Experience. *Journal of Psychedelic Studies*, 4(3), 171–78.

Mahmood, S. (2015). *Religious Difference in a Secular Age*: A Minority Report. Princeton, NJ: Princeton University Press.

Marinacci, M. (2023). *Psychedelic Cults and Outlaw Churches: LSD, Cannabis, and Spiritual Sacraments in Underground America*. Rochester, VT: Park Street Press.

Maroukis, T. C. (2010). *The Peyote Road: Religious Freedom and the Native American Church*. Norman, OK: University of Oklahoma Press.

Martin, C. (2014). *A Critical Introduction to the Study of Religion*. New York, NY: Routledge.

Masuzawa, T. (2005). *The Invention of World Religions Or, How European Universalism Was Preserved in the Language of Pluralism*. Chicago: University of Chicago Press.

McNally, M. (2009). *Honoring Elders: Aging, Authority, and Ojibwe Religion*. New York, NY: Columbia University Press.

Meier, L. (2007). RLUIPA and Congressional Intent. *Albany Law Review*, 70, 1435–40.

Metzner, R., ed. (2005). *Sacred Mushroom of Visions: Teonanácatl: A Sourcebook on the Psilocybin Mushroom*. Rochester, VT: Park Street Press.

Miller, M. J., Albarracin-Jordan, J., Moore, C., & Capriles, J. M. (2019). Chemical Evidence for the Use of Multiple Psychotropic Plants in a 1,000-Year-Old Ritual Bundle from South America. *Anthropology*, 116(23), 11207–12.

Mooney, J. (1896). The Mescal Plant and Ceremony. *Therapeutic Gazette* 12, 7–11.

Moore, R. L. (1987). *Religious Outsiders and the Making of Americans.* New York, NY: Oxford University Press.

Muhammad, K. G. (2010). *The Condemnation of Blackness: Race, Crime, and the Making of Modern Urban America.* Cambridge, MA: Harvard University Press.

Muraresku, B. C. (2020), *The Immortality Key: The Secret History of the Religion with No Name.* New York, NY: St. Martin's Press.

Myers, G. E. (2001). *William James His Life and Thought.* New Haven, CT: Yale University Press.

Nalewicki, J. (2022). Nazca child ingested psychoactive cactus just before ceremonial death in ancient Peru. *Live Science*, October 31. Accessed online, February 20, 2024. www.livescience.com/psychoactive–plants–peru–tro phy–head.

Neuman, G. L. (1997). The Global Dimensions of RFRA. *Constitutional Commentary*, 14(1), 33–54.

Nongbri, B. (2012). *Before Religion: A History of a Modern Concept.* New Haven, CT: Yale University Press.

Oroc, J. (2009). *Tryptamine Palace: 5-Meo-DMT and the Sonoran Desert Toad.* Rochester, VT: Park Street Press.

Osborn, J. M. (2004). RLUIPA's Land Use Provisions: Congress's Unconstitutional Response to City of Boerne. *Environs: Environmental Law and Policy Journal*, 28(1), 156–79.

Osmond, H. (1961). New techniques of investigation. In *Proceedings of Two Conferences on Parapsychology and Pharmacology.* New York, NY: Parapsychology Foundation, 76–8.

Osto, D. E. (2016). *Altered States: Buddhism and Psychedelic Spirituality in America.* New York, NY: Columbia University Press.

Pahnke, W. N. (1963). "Drugs and Mysticism: An Analysis of the Relationship between Psychedelic Drugs and the Mystical Consciousness." MA thesis, Harvard University.

Parenti, C. (1999). *Lockdown America: Police and Prisons in the Age of Crisis.* New York, NY: Verso.

Parsell, S. G. (1992). Revitalization of the Free Exercise of Religion under State Constitutions: A Response to *Employment Division v. Smith. Notre Dame Law Review*, 68(4), 747–74.

Pavlik, S. (1992). The U.S. Supreme Court Decision on Peyote in *Employment Division v. Smith*: A Case Study in the Suppression of Native American Religious Freedom. *Wicazo Sa Review*, 8(2), 30–9.

Priest, H. (2022). Personal correspondence with the author, Jan. 19, 2022.

Phelps, J., Shah, R. N., & Lieberman, J. A. (2022). The Rapid Rise in Investment in Psychedelics – Cart before the Horse. *JAMA Psychiatry*, 79(3), 189–90.

Pollan, M. (2018a). *How to Change Your Mind: What the New Science of Psychedelics Teaches Us about Consciousness, Dying, Addiction, Depression, and Transcendence*. New York, NY: Penguin Books.

Pollan, M. (2018b). How to Change Your Mind. Talks at Google. *YouTube*, June 19. Accessed January 15, 2024. www.youtube.com/watch?v=KuhmZSFvhL0&t=117s.

Pfaff, J. (2017). *Locked In The True Causes of Mass Incarceration-and How to Achieve Real Reform*. New York: Basic Books.

Richards, W. (2016). *Sacred Knowledge: Psychedelics and Religious Experiences*. New York, NY: Columbia University Press.

Richardson, R. D. (2006). *William James: In the Maelstrom of American Modernism*. Boston, MA: Mariner.

Richardson, J. T., & B. McGraw (2019). Congressional Efforts to Defend and Extend Religious Freedom and the Law of Unintended Consequences. *Journal for the Study of Beliefs and Worldviews* 20(1 & 2), 13–29.

Roper, L. (2010). Martin Luther's Body: The "Stout Doctor" and His Biographers. *The American Historical Review*, 115(2), 351–84.

Rosenthal, F. (1971). *The Herb: Hashish Versus Medieval Muslim Society*. Leiden: Brill.

Sacco, M. A., Zibett, A., Bonetta, C. F., Scalise, C., Abenavoli, L., Guarna, F., Gratteri, S., Ricci, P., & Aquila, I. (2022). Kambo: Natural Drug or Potential Toxic Agent? A Literature Review of Acute Poisoning Cases. *Toxicology Reports*, 9, 905–13.

Scheidegger, M. (2021). Comparative Phenomenology and Neurobiology of Meditative and Psychedelic States of Consciousness: Implications for Psychedelic-Assisted Therapy. In C. S. Grob & J. Grigsby (eds.), *Handbook of Medical Hallucinogens*. New York, NY: The Guilford Press, pp. 395–413.

Schilbrack, K. (2022). The Concept of Religion. *The Stanford Encyclopedia of Philosophy*, accessed January 15, 2024. https://plato.stanford.edu/archives/sum2022/entries/concept-religion.

Schoenfeld, H. (2018). *Building the Prison State Race and the Politics of Mass Incarceration*. Chicago, IL: Chicago University Press.

Shakman Hurd, E., & Sullivan, W. S., eds. (2021). *At Home and Abroad: The Politics of American Religion*. New York, NY: Columbia University Press.

Shults, L. F. (2022). Studying Close Entity Encounters of the Psychedelic Kind: Insights from the Cognitive Evolutionary Science of Religion. *The International Journal for the Psychology of Religion* 33(4), 1–15.

Smith, G. A. (2021). About Three-in-Ten U.S. Adults Are Now Religiously Unaffiliated. Pew Research Center, December 14. Accessed December 13, 2023. www.pewresearch.org/religion/2021/12/14/about-three-in-ten-u-s-adults-are-now-religiously-unaffiliated.

Smith, J. Z. (1982). *Imagining Religion: From Babylon to Jonestown*. Chicago, IL: University of Chicago Press.

Stoddard, B. (2023). Entheogens: Psychedelic Religion in the United States, Part Two, *Religion Compass* 17(10), 1–12.

Stoddard, B. (2024). Ayahuasca Tourism: Curating Authenticity in Transformative Times. *Nova Religio: The Journal of Alternative and Emergent Religions*, forthcoming.

Strassman, R. (2001). *DMT: The Spirit Molecule: A Doctor's Revolutionary Research into the Biology of Near-Death and Mystical Experiences*. Rochester, VT: Park Street Press.

Sullivan, W. F. (2009). *Prison Religion: Faith-Based Reform and the Constitution*. Princeton, NJ: Princeton University Press.

Sullivan, W. F. (2014). *A Ministry of Presence: Chaplaincy, Spiritual Care, and the Law*. Chicago, IL: University of Chicago Press.

Sullivan, W. F., Shakman Hurd, E., Mahmood, S., & Danchin, P. G., eds. (2015). *Politics of Religious Freedom*. Chicago, IL: University of Chicago Press.

Touw, M. (1981). The Religious and Medical Use of Cannabis in China, India, and Tibet. *Journal of Psychoactive Drugs*, 13(1), 23–34.

Useem, B., & A. M. Piehl (2008). *Prison State: The Challenge of Mass Incarceration*. New York, NY: Cambridge University Press.

Walsh, A. M. (2001). Religious Land Use and Institutionalized Persons Act of 2000: The Land Use Provisions Are Both Unconstitutional and Unnecessary. *William & Mary Bill of Rights Journal* 10(1), 189–215.

Wasson, R. G. (1957). Seeking the magic mushroom. *Life Magazine*, 49(19), 100–2, 109–20.

Wasson, R. G., Hofmann, A., & Ruck, C. A. P. (1978). *The Road to Eleusis: Unveiling the Secret of the Mysteries*. New York, NY: Harcourt, Brace, Jovanovich.

Wasson, R. G., Kramrisch, S., Ott, J., & Ruck, C. A. P. (1986). *Persephone's Quest: Entheogens and the Origins of Religion.* New Haven, CT: Yale University Press.

Wenger, T. (2009). *We Have a Religion: The 1920s Pueblo Indian Dance Controversy and American Religious Freedom.* Chapel Hill, NC: The University of North Carolina Press.

Williamson, S., & Sherwood A. (2023). Fungi Fiction: Analytical Investigation into the Church of Psilomethoxin's Alleged Novel Compound Using UPLC-HRMS. *ChemRxiv.* Accessed online, August 18, 2023. https://chemrxiv.org/engage/chemrxiv/article–details/64358de9736114c96352edf9.

Cambridge Elements ≡

New Religious Movements

Founding Editor

†James R. Lewis
Wuhan University

The late James R. Lewis was a Professor of Philosophy at Wuhan University, China.
He was the author or co-author of 128 articles and reference book entries, and
editor or co-editor of 50 books. He was also the general editor for the *Alternative Spirituality
and Religion Review* and served as the associate editor for the *Journal of Religion and
Violence*. His prolific publications include *The Cambridge Companion to Religion and
Terrorism* (Cambridge University Press 2017) and *Falun Gong: Spiritual Warfare
and Martyrdom* (Cambridge University Press 2018).

Series Editor

Rebecca Moore
San Diego State University

Rebecca Moore is Emerita Professor of Religious Studies at San Diego State University. She
has written and edited numerous books and articles on Peoples Temple and the
Jonestown tragedy. Publications include *Beyond Brainwashing: Perspectives on Cultic
Violence* (Cambridge University Press 2018) and *Peoples Temple and Jonestown in the
Twenty-First Century* (Cambridge University Press 2022). She is reviews editor
for *Nova Religio*, the quarterly journal on new and emergent religions published by the
University of Pennsylvania Press.

About the Series

Elements in New Religious Movements go beyond cult stereotypes and popular
prejudices to present new religions and their adherents in a scholarly and engaging
manner. Case studies of individual groups, such as Transcendental Meditation
and Scientology, provide in-depth consideration of some of the most well known, and
controversial, groups. Thematic examinations of women, children, science, technology,
and other topics focus on specific issues unique to these groups. Historical
analyses locate new religions in specific religious, social, political, and cultural contexts.
These examinations demonstrate why some groups exist in tension with the wider
society and why others live peaceably in the mainstream. The series highlights the
differences, as well as the similarities, within this great variety of religious expressions. To
discuss contributing to this series please contact Professor Moore.

Cambridge Elements ≡

New Religious Movements